C000100736

'*Love Beyond* is the extraordin[...]
like door-to-door visiting, bu[...]
thirty years, befriending hu[...]
maids and models in Soho, [...]
humour and disarming hon[...]
through this book we meet the kindness of Jesus; amazing, persevering, non-judgemental kindness, which sees and cares for each one. Thank you Heidi for your perseverance in loving, and for encouraging us with the telling of your story.'
Dawn Pointing (Spiritual Director)

'*Love Beyond* is a compelling read that I highly recommend to anyone who desires to overcome the obstacles they face in the pursuit of the call of God on their life. It will hold your interest, challenge your faith, engender compassion and encourage you to endure in whatever work the Lord Jesus has graciously committed into your hands.'
Rev Ray Michael Djan, ministry development mentor, Bible School lecturer and General Director of True Vine International Mission

'No hype, no exaggeration and no hubris. The honest story of the compassion of God towards women wrapped in the world of prostitution in London's red-light area. Told through the eyes of one lady, inspired by her faith to carry the message of grace and forgiveness to the brothels of Soho. Heidi tells it like it is; she doesn't pretend that it's easy. But what shines from the pages is the simple and powerful reality that God really cares for every person, whoever they are.'
Matt Frost, senior pastor at Cirencester Baptist Church and former pastor of City Gates Church, Soho

'Written with honesty, thoughtfulness and humour, *Love Beyond* shines a light on the lives of women who would otherwise be hidden and forgotten in the shadows of London's Soho district. Heidi's own life story and the stories of the women she has encountered over the last thirty years provide a compelling reminder that Jesus longs to be gracious to us and to pour out His love on us, if only we would let Him.'

Keziah Bowers, personal friend

LOVE
BEYOND

Bringing God's Love to Soho's Red-light District

HEIDI BAUMGARTNER

instant
apostle

First published in Great Britain in 2019

Instant Apostle

The Barn
1 Watford House Lane
Watford
Herts
WD17 1BJ

British Library Cataloguing-in-Publication Data

A catalogue record for this book is available from the British Library

This book and all other Instant Apostle books are available from Instant Apostle:

Website: www.instantapostle.com

E-mail: info@instantapostle.com

ISBN 978-1-909728-95-0

Printed in Great Britain

Contents

Some names have been changed to protect anonymity.

Acknowledgements

First I would like to thank two people whose names I don't recall but whom I met briefly during a retreat at the International House of Prayer (IHOP), Kansas City, in 2012. This man and woman obeyed Jesus and told me they had the impression God was saying that I was going to write a book. To be honest, when the man first told me this, I thought he was definitely mistaken, as I had never written more than quarterly newsletters. When a few weeks later a young woman told me the same thing, I was a bit more attentive, but still not very convinced and thought that if this was ever going to happen, it would certainly require a miracle from the Lord.

Secondly, I would like to thank my long-term mentor, Rev Ray Djan, who on several occasions reminded me of what the two people mentioned above had said, and who strongly encouraged me to make a go of it. I also want to take this opportunity to express my deep gratitude for all his prayers, godly wisdom, advice and valuable spiritual input during the last sixteen years. Ray and his wife, Susie, are senior pastors of True Vine Church and co-founders of Grace City Bible School in Croydon.

I would like to thank Max, Keziah, Jane and Christina who have encouraged me while writing and who have proofread some of the stories. I would especially like to thank Robert Ashworth who read through the book several times in an attempt to make sure that the manuscript was free from grammatical errors! Without Rob's help, the manuscript wouldn't have been as well presented and I'm very grateful for all the hours he's put in.

I would like to thank my family and friends in Switzerland, my friends and church family in City Gates, past and present, for their encouragement, prayer and financial support during the past thirty years. Without their help I wouldn't have been able to do this work and would therefore never have written this book.

I would like to thank Roger Forster for all the invaluable Bible teaching I've received under his ministry, and for taking the time to write a foreword to my book.

Lastly, I would like to thank the leadership team of City Gates Church for their kindness, as I've borrowed *Love Beyond* as the title for my book from the theme of our recent church weekend away in 2017.

Foreword
by Roger Forster

It was a privilege to have had Heidi in our fellowship for many years. She came first to our congregation, Ichthus Soho, when assigned by her Bible training college to join us for practical experience. Soho, as most of you will know, is the centre of London's sex trade. The Ichthus Christian Fellowship had planted a small but active church there a few years before. Heidi, with her calling on her life for service in such an area, plus her naivety and lack of experience, fitted in perfectly! However, her commitment, devotion and sacrifice for her Lord Jesus Christ were an inspiration and challenge to all of us in our various services for Christ.

Now it is also a privilege for me to be asked to write a few words as a foreword for her book. This work contains experiences Heidi has had and an innumerable number of people she has met and wishes to introduce to us, as it takes us by the hand, as it were, and leads us through her stories. The reader will find it hard to put the book down as they are guided through adventure after adventure of God's provision, guidance, protection, overruling and foreknowledge.

Many years ago a popular book was written called *Finding Men for Christ*.[1] Similarly, Heidi's book could be called *Finding (mostly) Women for Christ!* With love, friendship and prayer she has helped many hopeless and lost women to find that they possess souls in which treasures are residing, waiting for Christ's release and redemption.

As Heidi takes us into this world, filled so often and so much by lovelessness, emptiness, pain and enslavement, you will be touched, if not shocked. As she leads you behind shut doors of privation and often fear, you will be challenged. The words of the apostle Paul, 'What shall I do, Lord?' (Acts 22:10), will be squeezed from your lips. If you don't want disturbance to your life, stop reading now.

However, having said all that, this is still a good read with some great tales. Thank you, Heidi, for putting your work down on paper and your spirit and soul into print. We know whatever our response to these pages, we have met you and those you have loved and served and are the better for it.

Roger Forster
Founder and leader of Ichthus Christian Fellowship

---

[1] G F Dempster, Hodder & Stoughton, 1965.

Introduction

Love Beyond contains personal stories and testimonies from my almost thirty years of working as a missionary in Soho's red-light district. They are written from my own perspective, the way I remember them, and not necessarily in chronological order.

I've been doing this work with the full support of City Gates Church. The church was planted by Ichthus Christian Fellowship in partnership with Youth With A Mission (YWAM) in 1985, but became independent of its mother church in 2004. As a missionary, I have received financial support through a regular, monthly contribution from City Gates Church and through family and friends in Switzerland and England.

Love Beyond is a book for people of all ages and backgrounds. It seeks to encourage and remind the older believer that God's word will never return void and that we can fully trust in God's promises, despite not having seen their full manifestation yet; for those who are younger in the faith, never to give up on people, but through God's grace and help to persevere in loving them; and for the youngest believers, that God's kingdom is not instant but is inherited through faith and patience. Finally, for all those in full-time ministry, that being successful is being faithful to Jesus and doing the things He has told us to.

I don't claim that I can love beyond; I still struggle most days to put other people first. For me, 'loving beyond' doesn't come naturally, but it's a gift freely given by Jesus through the Holy Spirit, who lives and works in and through us. In fact, I believe that 'loving beyond' is impossible without the Holy Spirit ministering the love of Jesus through us.

I still remember my first outreach in Zürich, Switzerland, to people who lived in the drug culture. I had recently become a Christian and was part of an outreach team which was trying to minister to a wide range of people. One Saturday I was asked to join some team members who were going to the park where drug addicts were hanging out. I wasn't too keen, as this was totally out of my comfort zone and I felt scared and uneasy about it. Nevertheless, I decided to give it a try, and together we left for the park.

To this day I don't know how, but in the park I became separated from my team. After looking in vain for my team members, I found myself standing near a water fountain. A young girl and boy were sitting there talking, so I joined them. I can't remember the conversation we had, but suddenly I felt something like a river rushing through me and out of my body. I was a bit taken aback by the experience and was wondering what it was all about, when the boy said, 'We can feel that you love and care about us!'

I can say with absolute certainty that this emotion wasn't from me but from the Holy Spirit flowing through me to embrace those two young people with the love of Jesus, a love which personally I wasn't capable of giving.

In the same park, a few months later, I embraced a young woman who had AIDS and who was full of scabs and open sores. She broke out in tears saying that no one had touched her for months because of the way she looked. Naturally speaking, I would not have touched her either, but would have tried to ignore and walk around her like everyone else did. But, as in the previous story, suddenly the love of Jesus just compelled me to approach and embrace her.

Usually for me, 'loving beyond' doesn't just happen when I'm feeling His love flowing through me in a supernatural way, but mostly by simply obeying what Jesus told me to do so many years ago, even if I don't always feel like doing it:

> Love is patient, love is kind. It does not envy, it does not boast, it is not proud. It does not dishonour others, it is not self-seeking, it is not easily angered, it keeps no record of wrongs. Love does not delight in evil but rejoices with the truth. It always protects, always trusts, always hopes, always perseveres.
> *1 Corinthians 13:4-7*

Jesus said that if we loved Him we would obey His word. 'Loving beyond' is exactly that: obeying Jesus, and, as we do, He fills us with His Holy Spirit and His supernatural love in order that our families, friends and work colleagues, and other people's lives we touch, can experience the love of the Father through Jesus.

PART ONE

MY STORY

1. My Childhood

I was born in 1956 in a small rural village in the German-speaking part of Switzerland. I was the daughter of a single mother, and for the first four years of my life grew up with my cousin, who was also without a father, and with my four aunts and two uncles, at my grandparents' home in the country.

My grandparents were members of a 'free church' and brought their children up in the faith. The neighbours often looked upon them with suspicion, as at the time most people attended the Swiss state church. Their reputation was not helped by having two daughters who had come home pregnant from a year's work experience abroad!

While our mothers worked, my cousin and I were looked after by our grandmother and whoever else was at home. Looking at the many family photos of that time, I can say that my cousin and I had a happy life and received a lot of attention, especially while all our aunts were still living at home.

During the following three years, my two uncles and two of my aunts got married, and the rest of the family (my grandparents, my youngest aunt, my cousin and her mother and my mother and I), moved from the country to a nearby town. We lived in a large four-bedroom flat, and I still remember its layout because of its long corridor: my cousin and I used to slide along its polished floor, which I remember no one else found amusing, apart from the two of us!

Before I was four, my mother met a handsome man at her workplace, and, after a short time of dating, they married. I immediately took to my stepfather, and therefore moving house and leaving the rest of my family wasn't that difficult. I'm sure I must have missed everyone, especially my cousin, as we were like sisters. We still lived in the same village and one year later we moved again, and from then on we literally lived around the corner from one another until the day we each left home.

After my mother married I had three more siblings: two sisters and one brother. My father worked in a factory as a mechanic, within walking distance from where we lived. He would come home for lunch and afterwards take a short nap before going back to work. In the evenings he always had time for us children: he played on the living room floor with the little ones, and he would play a board game or cards with me. When I was old enough, he taught me how to play chess. My father was also very good at telling bedtime stories, and if we ran out of books he would invent some of his own. For the first thirteen years we didn't have a television, and when I wasn't playing with my father I was reading. I used to borrow up to four books a week from the library, my favourite ones being detective stories.

My mother was a housewife and always at home taking care of us. In contrast to my father, she didn't play with us very much. In the evenings she preferred knitting rather than playing board games or cards. She was also handy with her sewing machine, and when I was older she helped me sew my first dress. We weren't rich but we had everything we needed. My mother was careful with money and always managed to save enough for us to go on a two-week family holiday in the summer and later also a week in the winter. In the winter, of course, we went skiing, and in the summer we went on long and beautiful walks in the Alps or other mountains.

My parents attended the Swiss state church. For many years my father held the office of treasurer and taught in the Sunday school in a neighbouring village. When I was little, I used to accompany him most Sundays. I still remember how proud I felt, walking alongside him. He also played the piano and led our singing. When I reached school age I had to attend the Sunday school in our village and then later, in my early teens, I took classes to prepare for confirmation.

When I was fourteen our family life was suddenly struck and shaken by the death of one of my sisters. My first sister was born with an incurable heart condition and spent many months in hospital after her birth. The doctors who treated my sister told my parents that she wouldn't grow to be very old, but nevertheless she was always a very lively and happy child.

I wasn't at home on the morning when my mother found my sister, who had died during the night. I was at the hairdresser's, on a month's work experience, when I received the sad news. After the phone call I simply carried on working, as what had just happened did not seem to register in me. When I came home in the evening, my sister's bed was empty and she was gone. My last chance to see her was before the funeral in the chapel of rest, but I didn't go there as I wanted to remember her the way she was when I had last seen her alive.

As a family we didn't talk about my sister's death, and I somehow managed to block it out of my mind until many years later, when Jesus finally helped me to cry for my sister and to mourn. My younger brother and sister were deeply affected by her death. She used to play with them all the time; I was a teenager and too old, I thought, for playing with my younger siblings, as I had other things on my mind. I remember my little sister used to open the window to call out her dead sister's name, saying that it was time for her to come home for dinner.

Needless to say, my parents were devastated by her death. Of course, they knew what the doctors had said, but nevertheless her death came unexpectedly and as a shock. She was always full of life and no one would have ever guessed her condition unless they had been told.

Many years later, my mother told me that a few weeks before my sister died she had said to my mother that once she had finished her current bottle of medication (her prescription drugs) she would be well and wouldn't need to take medicine any longer. My mother told her that once she finished the bottle she would have to start a new one. It was on the day my sister finished the last drops of that bottle that she went to be with Jesus!

An outsider would have probably thought that my parents' marriage was harmonious. Yet when I got older I realised there was a lot of tension between them and they didn't get on that well. My stepfather was an affectionate and loving man, whereas my mother was more reserved and found it difficult to show love. She had been brought up very strictly, and the Christian fellowship my grandparents attended was legalistic, despite believing in the work and power of the Holy Spirit. The women weren't allowed to wear trousers, or cut their hair, or go to any kind of entertainment. When my mother came home pregnant, one of the conditions of my grandparents' support was that she had to be part of the fellowship again. She told me the elders of the church had required her to stand in front of the congregation and repent publicly of the sin she had committed.

My mother must already have felt wounded and broken because of what had happened to her with my biological father. Receiving grace and mercy from her parents' congregation, instead of being put to public shame, might have altered the course of her emotional life, and could have brought healing and restoration to her heart.

When I was older, out of curiosity rather than the need to know, I once asked her who my biological father was. She said he was Italian, but she couldn't remember anything else – not even his name. That answer made me even more curious, so I asked my grandparents. My grandfather said that at the time they had made some enquiries about him, but when they found out he was already married, they felt they shouldn't pursue the matter any further. I've always been OK with not knowing who my biological father was, as my stepfather was the best dad I could have ever wished for!

2. Life as an Adult

Despite growing up in a secure home, I became restless after I left school. I felt there was something missing in my life and I wanted to travel and find whatever it was. In order to travel and work at the same time, I decided to train as a hairdresser and began a three-year apprenticeship in a nearby village. The money I received as an apprentice was very little and I wasn't able to afford much. My parents provided for my essentials, but if I wanted to go out or buy something special, I had to save up for it.

In my first year as an apprentice I had a steady boyfriend and my life was relatively balanced. After that relationship ended, I started to go out clubbing with my cousin and we were out most Friday and Saturday nights. I remember that during the following two years, on several occasions I went to work on a Saturday morning straight from a late-night drinking club.

Despite my desire for a steady relationship, I always ended up choosing the wrong type of men. But even though my lifestyle wasn't exemplary, I worked and studied hard for my exams and graduated with high marks.

I qualified as a hairdresser six months before my eighteenth birthday. I already had a job lined up with a Swiss hairdresser in Guernsey for when I turned eighteen.

In the meantime I had to earn some money and I thought, 'Why not turn my hobby into cash and work in a nightclub?' I started working in a café in Zürich while looking for a job as a barmaid. I soon found work, but it turned out to be a dark and seedy place where topless dancers entertained customers. Although I was a frequent visitor to nightclubs, this kind of establishment was foreign to me and made me feel uneasy, but I thought, 'It's only for a few months,' and so I took the job. I worked on commission, and in order to make money I started drinking with customers and seducing them into buying me champagne.

During the six months before I left for Guernsey, I got to know a man whom I would fall in love with. I met Mark in one of the late-night drinking clubs where I usually went after I finished work. We only had a couple of months to get to know each other, but I was head over heels in love and wondered how I was going to survive a year without seeing him. I knew, though, that it would be good for me to leave, because he was married and had several women, including his wife, working for him in prostitution. We didn't have much time together, and before I left he said that maybe we could pick up the relationship again once I came back from abroad.

There is a saying – 'out of sight, out of mind'. I didn't forget Mark that quickly, but I knew we wouldn't have a future. So once I was in Guernsey, I concentrated on my new job and learning English. For the first six months I lived in my boss' house near the seaside, where I had a nice room on the top floor, across from his daughter's room. We were about the same age and we got on well, but she wasn't a girl who went clubbing.

Once my English improved, I went out most evenings and therefore I thought it better to move out. I rented a single room in a shared house in the small town where I worked, and continued to work as a hairdresser. The strong desire to work at night eventually won me over and I left my job to work behind the bar at a disco.

I lived in Guernsey for a little more than a year. During that time I had several relationships with young men, but none of them were good.

Once I was back in Switzerland I gave up on the idea of working as a hairdresser. Although I was fully trained, I felt I lacked confidence and the artistic flair to know which hairstyle suited whom. Also, the hours were long and the money was bad. In any case, the night beckoned and I decided to continue to work as a barmaid, at least for a while. I loved the nightlife and was attracted by its different vices. I loved wearing nice clothes, especially those that would draw the attention of men.

My first job back in Switzerland was in an exclusive private nightclub in a hotel in Zürich. After a few weeks of working there I happened to see Mark by chance, and our relationship resumed. He said that his extravagant lifestyle required a lot of money and that, unless I worked as a call girl, we wouldn't be able to have a life together. I said I couldn't reconcile myself to the idea of selling my body, so he said that for the time being I could be his girlfriend. I didn't see him much, as he had obligations to his wife and the other women who worked for him. I knew he was fond of me, and because I knew about the other girls he didn't

27

need to pretend that I was the only one in his life. I was free too to have other relationships, as long as he didn't know the man I was sleeping with.

After working and living in Zürich for a little more than a year I decided it was time to move on. It was too difficult for me to be involved with a man I loved but with whom I had no future.

I moved to Geneva, in the French part of Switzerland, with the intention of learning French. For several months I worked in the bar of a first-class hotel, but decided after a discussion with a friend to change my job. He was a wealthy banker and used to say that no respectable businessman would ever marry a barmaid. I thought he had a point and decided it was time to change. I soon found a job as an administrator in a car rental firm, where I worked for two years. At the same time I enrolled at a private college to do a part-time course in secretarial work.

Although I worked in an office for two years, the nightlife didn't give up on me. I had a friend who managed a champagne bar, and when she was short of hostesses I would help her out. I didn't really enjoy entertaining and drinking with men, but somehow I seemed to get sucked back into a lifestyle that I didn't really want. A similar thing was true with men: I would have liked a lasting relationship but I always met men who were either married or not the marrying kind.

After I had lived in Geneva for three years and without my French having improved much (I spoke German or English most of the time), I moved to Montpellier in France where I studied French at a university for nine months.

I was nearly twenty-five when my studies in Montpellier drew to a close, but I didn't feel ready to move back to Switzerland. I was still feeling restless and was searching for something more in life. It wasn't just a lasting relationship I was looking for, but also something I couldn't put a name to.

During the time I lived in Geneva and Montpellier, I never lost touch with my family and visited them on several occasions. I would also visit my grandparents, my aunts and, of course, my cousin. My grandparents were strong believers in Jesus and I knew they had prayed for me every day since the day I was born.

On one of my visits, my grandparents gave me a yellow book called *Jesus our Destiny*, by Wilhelm Busch,[2] which I took with me to France. A few weeks before finishing my studies in Montpellier, I started to read the book. While I was reading it I was suddenly struck by the realisation that if I died that night I wouldn't go to heaven, as I wasn't saved. I had always thought myself a Christian but I realised that being baptised and confirmed wasn't enough. I decided to go to church, but the only one I found was a Catholic congregation, which I visited a couple of times.

A few weeks before I was due to leave Montpellier I accepted a job in Corsica, a small island off the south of France, where I wanted to continue to improve in the language. Once I arrived in Corsica I started my new job in a small bar in the principal town of Ajaccio. I also visited the big Catholic cathedral a couple of times but found it

---

[2] For English translation, see Amazon: Collection IPS, fourth edition, 1993.

boring and irrelevant. I decided that God and Jesus was for old people and that I would give my life to Him once I was sixty – or at least, after I had lived my life the way I wanted to.

After a few weeks of working in that bar, a friend of my boss was in need of a barmaid and asked if I would work for him. He was the owner of a cabaret, a nightclub not far from where I worked. The nightlife with all its vices beckoned again. By that time my visa to live in France had run out, and as I would never have received a work visa, I worked illegally. The cabaret was open late and I worked from about nine in the evening until four or five in the morning. The club's main entertainment was striptease and we usually had two female dancers and one male, a transvestite.

I also made friends with another couple of girls who worked at a friend's bar. Corsica had a wonderful, mild climate, although it was very hot during the summer months. During the day we would often go to the beach, and on our day off we usually went clubbing or visiting another friend's bar. I earned good money, cash in hand; I had a nice apartment and bought my first car. Life seemed to be good, at least from the outside, but it was certainly true in my case that 'all that glitters is not gold'.

Some of the nightclubs in Corsica were run by the Mafia, and my boss and some of his friends were part of this 'underworld'. My boss and his brother would always carry guns, and I knew they wouldn't hesitate to use them. On one occasion my boss had a disagreement with one of his friends who had recently finished his sentence in prison, having been convicted of murder. After the dispute his friend left angrily, but came back an hour or so later with his wife. Each was carrying a rifle. He shot into the air, commanded us all to line up and pointed his rifle at us.

This incident was very scary and we were all afraid; at least, the staff were. My boss eventually managed to appease him and they left the club to sort out their problem elsewhere.

This incident certainly shocked me, but it wasn't enough to make me leave as I seemed to have developed a taste for danger. I eventually did leave Corsica, not out of fear but because of my many unhappy relationships with men.

Back in Zürich I picked up from where I had left off nearly five years earlier. I returned to work in the exclusive private nightclub, and to a non-committal relationship with Mark.

After working there for almost a year, and at around twenty-seven years of age, I had the most unusual experience. I was standing behind the bar watching what was going on when suddenly it felt like I had just woken up from a deep sleep. I started to look around me and began to think that what I was doing was wrong. I had never felt like that before, and the next day I handed in my resignation and left after my contract terminated.

I didn't speak to anyone about that experience as I couldn't understand or explain it myself. After I left the club, I got a job in a good restaurant where I learned to serve delicious food and decant expensive wines. I hoped that in a couple of years I could become a manager of a restaurant as by then I would have had enough experience of bar and restaurant work. During this time my relationship with Mark continued, and I didn't expect anything to change. He really was the only man I had ever wanted.

The 'yellow book' was still in my possession, and a few months before my thirtieth birthday I read it again. One evening in my living room I said to God that if He really existed He would need to show me. I had learned from the book that Jesus would speak to people, and I figured that if this was true He could speak to me too. At the time I was concerned about living right, so I asked Jesus to show me His commandments in the Bible. I was looking for them but couldn't find them, and in a moment of desperation I decided just to open the book at random. Lo and behold, there they were, listed one after the other.

This took me rather by surprise, but something much deeper happened inside me: I instantly knew, without a shadow of a doubt, that God was real and that Jesus was very much alive. I also knew my relationship with Mark was wrong and that it couldn't go on. To walk away, of course, was easier said than done as I had failed several times not to go back to him, and I felt the situation was hopeless. I talked to Jesus about it, saying I knew the relationship was wrong and that I needed His help to leave Mark. The minute I admitted it was wrong and that I needed His help, something supernatural happened. It felt like something broke and shifted inside me, and for the first time ever in my adult life, I felt free!

So, a couple of weeks after I gave my life to Jesus I called Mark and said I had become a believer in Jesus and therefore couldn't see him any more. I didn't know what I was expecting, but his response surprised me. He said that if that was what really made me happy, I should go for it. Since then I haven't seen or heard from Mark, and I'm very much aware of the fact that this is God's amazing grace!

3. A New Life in Jesus

After I gave my life to Jesus, I felt at peace and I realised I had finally found what I had been looking for. At first, I continued to work at the restaurant, but because of the long hours and working weekends I handed in my notice. I didn't know what to do, so I asked Jesus to guide me and to help me find some other work. I applied for a few office jobs and, despite my lack of experience, I soon found work as a secretary in a big company. I also started to attend a church, a Christian fellowship which had been recommended to me by someone working for the Salvation Army. My new life with Jesus was good; I enjoyed going to my church and I also liked my new job.

I expected my parents to be happy for me too, as I had finally managed, with the help of Jesus, to change the course of my life. My mother didn't say much but was pleased that I had found a good job, but I had never seen my father so upset and angry. He blamed my grandparents, saying they had brainwashed me to go to one of their churches. My father didn't like 'free churches', one of the reasons being that my grandfather used to press him into joining the 'free church', which he adamantly refused to do. My father believed in God and was faithful to the traditional Swiss church, which I didn't want to go to. As a young believer I had a lot of zeal but not much wisdom, and unfortunately some of the discussions I had with my father following my conversion weren't very helpful.

My life totally changed, and as I was working normal office hours I had a lot of time on my hands. As well as attending the Sunday service I went to a midweek Bible study and a weekly outreach, where a small group of us would sing and preach on the streets. That I was a new creation in Jesus was evident, but there were lots of things I had to relearn. For example, I had to learn how to behave towards men and how not to dress to draw attention. I still remember a funny incident where I bought a new skirt, making sure that it wasn't too tight, but then got stuck with my heel in the floor of the tram, as I still wore rather high stilettos!

During my first year of being a Christian I also met a group of people who volunteered with an interdenominational ministry. Apart from singing and preaching on the streets, they reached out to drug users and homeless people. The couple who led the ministry rented a shop in Zürich which was called *Dä Wääg* meaning 'The Way'. *Dä Wääg* consisted of a bookshop and a basement room where they held services. Every Saturday a group of them would meet for prayer and then go out on to the streets to talk to people and invite them back to a service. First there would be a meal and then someone would preach, followed by people praying for each other and having fellowship.

I very much wanted to be part of that group and asked the leader if I could join them. He was happy for me to be part of their team, but first I needed the permission of the pastor of the church I had been attending since becoming a believer. I asked my pastor if it was OK for me to join the Saturday outreach team and he was happy for me to do so. However, the elders of the church weren't so keen. *Dä Wääg* was an interdenominational group of Christians which welcomed people with different Christian doctrines or beliefs, as long as they loved Jesus. At the time I thought every Christian believed the same thing, so I couldn't really understand their objections or concerns.

My office job was easy-going. I worked regular hours and the rest of the time I spent getting to know Jesus better and spending time with my new Christian friends. I loved going to church, attending Bible studies and reaching out to people to tell them about Jesus. I was fully involved and committed to church and to the Saturday group I was working with.

I was a very keen Christian with lots of enthusiasm and energy. I was certain I wanted to become a missionary and go and work somewhere where people didn't yet know Jesus. With the help of a friend from church, I started to make enquires about Bible schools in Switzerland, Germany and England. After viewing and having an interview with one Bible school in Switzerland and one in England, I decided to attend Redcliffe Bible college in Chiswick, London. My pastor and church fully supported me and I was looking forward to going about a year later. Very early on in my walk with Jesus I started to realise that I also had an enemy, and that Satan wasn't happy about me following Jesus. I had a couple of strange experiences in which beings I couldn't see, but could certainly feel, visited my bedroom at nights. This scared me and I asked at *Dä Wääg* if someone could pray for me as my church didn't believe in such occurrences. After I was prayed for, the nightly visits stopped.

I also started to have occasional thoughts of suicide, especially when standing at a train station. Once I had a strange urge to end my life by throwing myself under the approaching train. This incident really shocked me, and I asked the leader of *Dä Wääg* for help. He arranged for me to be prayed for and receive some ministry. During this time of prayer, I experienced some unusual manifestations and was set free in the name of Jesus from various unclean spirits who were still trying to hold on to my life.

With friends from *Dä Wääg* I attended a conference in Germany called 'Catch the Fire', led by evangelist Reinhard Bonnke. There I learned many things about the Holy Spirit and also about the gift of speaking in tongues, a prayer language which God gives to those who ask. I asked God for this but it was a few months until I was finally able to pray to Him in that prayer language. The elders of my church believed that the gifts of the Holy Spirit were only for the Early Church and that speaking in tongues was from the devil, which of course confused me somewhat. But the subject of the gift of tongues is addressed by the apostle Paul in chapter 14 of his first letter to the Corinthian church, where he instructs and teaches the people how to use the gift properly.

I also had the opportunity to attend a meeting in Austria. During the meeting, the speaker felt he had received a word from God. He said he had the impression Jesus wanted to bring some deeper healing to some people in the room whose birth hadn't been humanly planned and whose life had therefore nearly been terminated. I knew instantly that this man was speaking about me.

While I was training as a hairdresser I once thought I was pregnant. I didn't hesitate to tell my mother that if the test was positive I would certainly terminate the pregnancy. When we discussed the subject further, my mother admitted that she too had considered an abortion when she was pregnant with me, but the doctor she was seeing refused to do it.

The speaker of the meeting asked the people whom this word concerned to come to the front for prayer. Many people stood up to go forward, but when I wanted to get up from my seat I had an unusual experience. I suddenly saw myself in an operating theatre, witnessing a birth. I knew immediately that I was the child being born. There was also a male figure standing nearby, observing the birth, and once the child came out from its mother he received it into his arms and embraced it.

The moment the male figure, who I believe was Jesus, embraced the child, I experienced the most amazing liberation and freedom. It was as if an immense wall in my heart simply collapsed and disintegrated. The knowledge that Jesus had been there at my birth, receiving me into the world, was absolutely wonderful and started a healing process in my life.

Before that experience I had no idea that my being born without a father was even an issue. My stepfather was the best father I could ever have wished for. Nevertheless, it seemed my heart had been wounded even before I was born, and that I had deep-seated feelings of abandonment and rejection. It makes me wonder how much those deep-seated issues had actually affected the course of my life.

About six months before I was scheduled to leave for England, the elders of my church told me I needed to either cut my ties with *Dä Wääg* or leave the church. They felt that the doctrinal differences were too big to bridge and that if I continued to have fellowship there I would be a bad influence on others in the church. That was a bit of a shock, but after thinking about it I decided to keep going to *Dä Wääg*. The ministry wasn't registered as a church but as a Christian charity, and had a regular midweek meeting for discipleship and lots of prayer and fellowship. I concluded that if I wanted to help people like me and others who didn't have a straightforward background, I would be better off having fellowship with people who believed in the gifts and the power of the Holy Spirit in the now. *Dä Wääg* couldn't guarantee any financial support in my upcoming adventure in England but they said they would certainly support me in prayer, which they did for many years till their ministry finally closed.

4. Soho and How it All Began

Before I started Bible college in October 1988, I thought it would be good for me to improve my English as it didn't include any Christian vocabulary. With the help of a friend I found a six months' placement with a mission organisation called Worldwide Evangelisation for Christ (WEC), which at the time was based in Gerrards Cross, Buckinghamshire. I was one of many voluntary workers and helped with cleaning and cooking. Domestic work wasn't something I naturally enjoyed, but it was all a good learning experience and I enjoyed living among these men and women who had given up their usual jobs to work for the Lord. I met several missionaries passing through WEC on furlough and listened to their testimonies of working abroad, and I became sure that one day I too would be going to the ends of the earth!

On one occasion I was able to accompany a couple of full-time workers to a missions' conference in Keswick in the Lake District. WEC had a stall there, and the two women I was with were helping people with enquiries about mission and working with WEC. I was free to go to all the meetings, which of course I very much enjoyed. In one of the evening meetings I had an experience in which

I was no longer aware of my surroundings, but instead was totally immersed in what I saw and felt.

In the vision I saw the expanse of an ocean and hands stretching out from its waves. After a while those hands started to sink and disappear and, as I looked on, my heart cried out to God, saying, 'No! Please bring those hands back!' Then the scene changed and I saw a very big, bright light to my left. To my right I saw women dressed as prostitutes in the way I knew them from home, wearing miniskirts with over-the-knee boots. To my surprise, the women started to take off their clothes. Then I saw a pair of hands which handed them a clean, white robe, which the women took and dressed themselves with. Then the vision ended and I became aware again of the speaker sharing his message.

This experience left me with some questions, but I understood that the bright light represented God's throne or presence, and the white robes His righteousness, the free gift of salvation! At the time I didn't share the vision with anyone but left it with the Lord. I knew from many testimonies I'd heard that things don't always happen overnight, and that Jesus would guide me and give me more insight and understanding when the time was right.

At the end of the six months I left WEC having been inspired and encouraged by the many people who worked there or had passed through.

I enrolled at Redcliffe Bible college in Chiswick, London, in the autumn of 1988. Redcliffe was a missionary training college which offered a two-year course in cross-cultural mission and usually only took students who were planning to work abroad. I didn't know where I was going but I hoped it would be far away, on a different continent. The majority of the students were from England, but there was a female student from Germany and another one from Switzerland. There was also a young woman from China, one from Malaysia and one from Japan, and a couple of young men from South Korea. It was a good mix and therefore already very cross-cultural!

Our training wasn't only academic but also practical, and every student was placed with a local church in London. I asked if I could be placed with a church from Ichthus Christian Fellowship, as this had been recommended to me by a woman at WEC. She thought that while at college I should continue reaching out to people, as it seemed this was one of the gifts God had given me. She believed that Ichthus would be able to help me improve and develop that gift. The college agreed, and I wrote a letter to the Ichthus office. After a while they responded, saying that I should get in touch with the pastor of City Gates, a small church plant in Soho.

At that time I didn't know anything about Soho, and it certainly came as a surprise when I found out that it was a place where women worked in prostitution. In the letter to Ichthus I hadn't mentioned anything about the vision I had had, but it seemed that God was already opening an unexpected door.

The college didn't want me to do the placement by myself and arranged for another student to join me. I was accompanied by Judy, a second-year student who wanted to go to Thailand to work among girls in the sex trade, which she did once she finished college.

I will always remember that day when I first went with Judy to Soho. Once we arrived at Piccadilly Circus we walked up Shaftesbury Avenue, then turned left into Rupert Street. Walking up Rupert Street we passed some clubs where girls stood in the open doors, trying to call in customers. We also passed a couple of signs reading 'peep show' and 'models'.

While I was walking alongside Judy I felt very confident. I remember thinking and saying to Jesus in my heart, 'Oh, I know all about this kind of life!' and Jesus responding in my heart saying, 'Heidi, you don't know anything!'

At that time City Gates was a small church in the heart of Soho and had been planted in 1985 by Ichthus and YWAM in partnership. When Judy and I joined, the majority of its people were students, and there were a few people in their early thirties. I immediately enjoyed going to City Gates as it very much reminded me of *Dä Wääg*. Most people in the church were involved in outreach, either visiting the homeless or doing a weekly outreach in Soho. On Friday evenings people would go out to worship and preach on the streets and also visit some of the red-light flats and clubs. Judy and I would usually do our placement once a week in an afternoon, and we would also attend the church service on the Sunday.

The pastor of City Gates introduced us to our task ahead, and Judy and I started to do door-to-door visits in the red-light district. At around the same time as Judy and I began our placement, several people from City Gates moved on to the London Borough of Pimlico to plant another church. Unfortunately, among those leaving were some who used to visit the red-light flats.

I vividly recall our first visit together. We were walking down Berwick Street and knocking on a couple of walk-up flats. I was already feeling disheartened and discouraged after a few people had shouted from behind closed doors, telling us to go away. I've never liked doing door-to-door visits and I remember asking Jesus, in one of my very first evangelistic endeavours, never to ask me again to do door-to-door visits! But being new in Soho, there was no way into the women's flats apart from knocking on their doors!

At the time I didn't have much confidence that we would get into any of the flats, but Jesus was gracious. At the flat which we had decided beforehand was going to be the last one for that particular day, a woman opened the door and invited us in. We found out that the flat had previously been visited by people from City Gates Church, and that the women were quite happy for us to come and have a chat.

The woman who opened the door was the 'maid'. This is the person who lets the clients in when the 'model', the sex worker, is busy. She also does the housework and the cooking. The 'maid' is usually hired by the person running the flat, called 'the madam', or by the 'model' herself.

The red-light flats are usually on the first and second floors of a two- or three-storey building and therefore called 'walk-up flats'. The main entrance is always open, and signs saying 'models' point the way to the flats upstairs. They are usually one-bedroom apartments and, depending on their size, we would sit either in the kitchen or the living room, which is also where the clients would wait for their turn to be served.

During our first year this flat became our weekly encouragement, as at many of the other flats we tried to visit the women would usually just shout 'busy' from behind the closed doors. There were two maids and two models who worked on a fortnightly basis, and the four of them were kind and helpful and appreciated our visits.

For me it was also a season of learning: how not to be distracted by any noises coming from the bedroom; how to pick up again on a discussion as though the model had never left the room; how not to feel naked or exposed while being lusted after by a waiting customer; and how to pray often and silently in tongues, the prayer language God had given me. I can only thank Jesus for those four women whom over time I got to know very well, and whom I visited for many years till each one of them left Soho for one reason or another.

After we had been visiting the flats in Soho for a year, Judy graduated from Bible school. I started my second year at college and asked if I could continue my placement with City Gates. It wasn't the norm for a student to stay on the same placement for two years, as the college encouraged students to have a range of work experiences. I, though, felt very strongly that I had found my calling and that I should continue my placement in Soho, and, after some discussion with my tutor, I received permission to stay at City Gates. Unfortunately, the college wasn't able to replace Judy as there was no one else who felt called to work among sex workers, so I continued the placement by myself.

I've never felt afraid visiting the flats on my own. I was very aware of God's protection and believed He would look after me, and I had nothing to fear. It was a challenge, though, knocking on all those doors every week and being turned away by the majority of the women. But, as always, God was merciful, and He opened two additional flats for me to visit weekly.

In one of these flats two women, the maid and model, were particularly open and friendly. We used to read the Bible together and the maid especially was keen to learn more. The model was often busy and had to attend to her clients. Jesus gave me a good relationship with both women and in the course of time they invited me to their homes, introduced me to their families and friends, and cooked me delicious Sunday roast dinners.

The model was the same age as me – thirty-three at the time – and had been working in prostitution since the age of thirteen. She had been brought up in foster care from which she had run away several times, and finally ended up in Soho where she first started to sell her body on the street. Despite being rejected and treated unjustly by her family, she had a big and compassionate heart. I always found her helping other people less fortunate than herself and who were either in some sort of need or in trouble.

After more than twenty-eight years we're still friends and in regular contact with each other. In a recent conversation she told me that the first time she ever had hope that there could be a different life for her was after she had met me. She stopped working in the sex industry many years ago but is still helping people. She recently opened a second-hand shop whose profit will be used to help young people take a different path to the one she took.

A few months before I graduated from Bible school, the pastor of City Gates asked if I would consider working full-time with the church once I finished my studies. During the two years there I had got to know several people from the church, and it felt like a big family to me.

There was nothing else I wanted to do. I felt a strong calling from the Lord to reach out to women working in prostitution, not just anywhere but particularly in Soho.

Leaving Bible school was a bit sad as I had to say goodbye to some people I cared very much for. One of my best friends was from Japan and went back home to do some mission work in her own country, and of course Judy was preparing to go to Thailand. Bible school was a very special and precious time for me. I learned a lot about the God of the Bible, and it was a great privilege to have been able to spend two years studying like that. I graduated having passed all my tests and finished all my essays. I left college full of zeal and vision and couldn't wait to start full-time in Soho.

First, though, I had to go back to Switzerland to apply for a religious visa for England. Switzerland wasn't in the EU and I needed a visa to work with City Gates. It took a few months, which of course seemed like ages, but it was good for me to catch up with my family and with my friends from *Dä Wääg*. It was an encouragement to know that they fully stood with me and supported me in their prayers.

Once I received my visa I was off to England again, saying goodbye to family and friends, but it would never

be for long as I have usually visited Switzerland every
year.

PART TWO

1990-2000

5. Starting Out Full-time

For the first two years I shared a flat in Soho with some other women from the church. The two-bed maisonette in Soho's Berwick Street was managed by Green Light, a project of City Gates Church, to help finance the work with the homeless. Green Light also rented a house in New Oxford Street, which was used as a community house where people who had been on the streets lived with people from our church fellowship. The two-bed maisonette in Berwick Street was on the first and second floor, while the room on the ground floor was used for other church activities. One of those activities was a Saturday drop-in café which provided hot meals for the homeless.

It was a good flat-share and I have fond memories of that time. My flatmates were mainly students and therefore changed a couple of times. We held a weekly Bible study and had more or less an open door to whoever wanted to drop in. One of the students I shared with also helped with the red-light work, but, no matter who lived in the flat, each flatmate was supportive in welcoming the few women who came to visit.

We all lived simple lives as none of us had much money. In fact, I was often down to my last 50p and wondering where my next meal was going to come from. During the first two years I lived rent-free as the project covered that expense, and for this I was very grateful. For the rest of my expenses I had to learn to trust God.

In hindsight, it's very interesting to note that one of the first things Jesus taught me was about giving. About a year after I became a Christian I was reading through the book of Malachi in the Bible, the third chapter of which talks about tithing. As I was reading I felt very strongly that God wanted me to start giving a tithe, 10 per cent of my gross income. That was a bit of a shock, as I liked to keep hold of my money and I was also saving to go to Bible school. I didn't know then the theological arguments about tithing, but I just obeyed. As far as I understand it, the debate about tithing centres on it being an Old Testament law, and that because Jesus has set us free from the obligations of keeping that law, tithing is no longer necessary. Anyway, I started to tithe and still do, and I believe that, even though tithing is from the Old Covenant, the benefits of the promise in Malachi still remain.

Having no salary, I had to ask God for clothes, shoes, food, travel expenses, etc. I freely admit it was a challenge and very often still is. From the beginning I told Jesus that if I worked for Him then He would have to provide for me without me having to ask people for money. I don't think it's wrong to ask, but I felt that the provision for my finances should be met by asking only Him.

One of the ways Jesus provided for me while I lived in Berwick Street was through a woman I used to visit. The house we lived in was joined by a small, low roof to one of the flats I visited. The roof could be accessed from our staircase window and led to the kitchen window of the other flat. I had good relationships with the women who worked there, especially with one of the maids. She also happened to be a very good cook, and every time I was about to run out of food her kitchen window would open and she would call with a loud voice, 'Heidi, I have cooked too much food today! Would you like to come and take some for yourself?'

Several years later I told her how God used to provide for me through her cooking. As she was listening, she became very moved and tears welled up in her eyes.

But not all provision was from the Lord, and the following incident still makes me smile when I think about it. It happened very early on and shows some of my naivety. It was at a time when I didn't have much money, but needed some new underwear.

I was visiting one of the flats where I knew the women well. We were talking when someone knocked on the door. The maid opened it and a young girl carrying an enormous bag came in. The girl opened the bag and it was full of beautiful knickers and bras. I thought to myself, 'Wow, what an amazing answer to prayer!' The four of us looked through the vast number of knickers and bras, and eventually I selected a couple for myself. Not only were they pretty but they were also much cheaper than in any of the shops. The maid and model also bought some.

After the girl left, the maid looked at me sternly and said, 'Heidi, I don't think you should have bought any of these. You are a Christian and these are stolen!'

I said, 'Thank you for telling me now! Why didn't you say something before?'

She replied that she thought I knew.

Yes, I knew that people – especially those addicted to drugs – would sell stolen goods, but there were also a couple of wholesalers who would visit the flats with merchandise. When I saw the huge amount the girl was carrying I thought that it couldn't have been stolen, as no one could have taken that many bras and knickers!

I thought the whole incident was rather funny, but I promised myself that I would be sure not to buy anything like this ever again. I told my pastor of my misguided conduct, in confidence, I thought, but soon afterwards it became an inside joke in the church that I was wearing stolen underwear!

I had to learn to trust Jesus not only for daily provision, but also for daily courage. There was one particular flat which I always found very difficult to go to. I couldn't understand why anyone would want to go there. The flat was in a basement and its staircase was narrow and dingy. Whenever I knocked on the door, an unfriendly woman would open it with a scary–looking Rottweiler behind her.

Normally I'm not afraid of dogs, but this one didn't inspire me with much confidence! Neither did the woman who opened the door. When I knocked, she would pull it open and, with an angry look, say, 'Oh, it's you again. Go away!'

I would have been very happy never to go back there, but Jesus compelled me time and time again. Before descending the dingy staircase, I would pluck up courage by walking several times around the block, praying, preparing myself for another very unfriendly 'go away' and hoping that the dog had already had his dinner.

This scenario repeated itself, I can't remember exactly how many times, but probably for about a year. Then one day after opening the door, she looked at me and said, 'It's not you again ... Come in and tell me what you want!' I can't remember what I said but from that day on I visited her every week till the flat eventually closed many years later.

Several people worked in that basement: the woman who opened the door, her brother, her female partner and two models. Everyone was very friendly towards me and seemed to be happy for me to visit. Even the dog turned out to be less scary than he looked. It was a huge turn of events, and of course only Jesus could have orchestrated anything like that!

In that flat we read the Bible and prayed, watched a video with an evangelistic message and had many different discussions about Jesus. I was also invited into their homes and to a big family party up north. One of the models visited me for a week in Switzerland during my annual family holiday, and the other one eventually, after many years, gave her life to Jesus.

6. Living on the Third Floor of a Brothel

After sharing a flat for nearly two years in Berwick Street, the Green Light Project closed and I had to look for accommodation elsewhere. I believed that God wanted me to live in Soho, but humanly speaking this was totally impossible as I didn't have the finances to do so. Nevertheless, I insisted that if Jesus wanted me to live in Soho He was somehow going to provide. In the meantime, I had friends who offered me a bed as a short-term solution. Essentially I needed a miracle, and there was absolutely nothing I could do about it but wait and pray. Jesus was really gracious, and He provided a flat after only a three months' wait.

One of the maids I knew took on two new flats in Great Windmill Street just opposite Soho Primary School. She said that the flat on the third floor was empty and if I wanted it she would make some enquiries. Apparently only two working flats are permitted per building and that was the reason the third-floor flat was empty. She asked the leaseholder whether I could rent it, but unfortunately he had already let it to someone else. A few weeks later, the person who had intended to rent the flat was arrested and had to go to prison, and so it was free for me to move into.

The maid told the leaseholder, Gerald, that I didn't have much money and that I needed a low rent. After some negotiation he agreed to £70 a week, which was a miracle! The flat needed a lot of work done to it and Gerald offered me one month rent-free to sort everything out. My church friends moved into action: someone painted, another person rewired the electricity, and someone else fitted new carpets. One of the Ichthus churches provided a plumber who fitted a new toilet, and someone else called in a friend who was able to fix the leaking roof.

Gerald asked how I was going to pay for my rent, as he knew I didn't earn any money. I said that I would have to pray every week and ask Jesus for it. He gave me a look that said, 'Are you kidding me?' but he didn't go back on his word. As a testimony to God's glory and Jesus' faithfulness, I can say that every month when Gerald came to collect the rent I had the money. There were two occasions when I didn't have the full amount on the day he usually collected it. I said to Jesus that I couldn't tell Gerald that I hadn't got the money, as I'd told him that He, Jesus, would provide it. On both occasions Gerald phoned to say that he couldn't make it that day and that he would pick it up on another day. By the time he came to collect the rent Jesus had provided the money, and for ten years Gerald never walked away empty-handed.

The house I lived in was old and had no central heating. The women downstairs used only electric heaters whereas I heated the living room with one of those old gas fires that needed a gas bottle. There was quite a draught and in the cold weather I used to 'double glaze' the windows with a plastic sheet which could be bought for that purpose. During the winter I had to order several gas bottles, and on one occasion I was about to run out of not only gas, but also money. Two days earlier someone had given me a cheque, but I had no cash available to pay for the gas bottle I had ordered. I thought that although I had once told Jesus that I would never borrow money, it wouldn't really be borrowing as I did have some, just not in cash. I said to myself that there was nothing else to do but borrow it, as there was no way I would have cash by the following day when I had to pay for that gas bottle.

I can't remember if it was the same afternoon or the next morning, but the doorbell rang and I received an unexpected visit from a couple from Switzerland. I didn't know them, and after I invited them in they explained why they had come to see me.

In Switzerland a few weeks earlier they had had new carpets fitted in their house. The man who had done the work was a friend of mine, called Christian. As it happened, they started to talk, and in the conversation they mentioned that they were going to visit London for a few days. Christian said he had a friend living in Soho who worked as a missionary and asked if they wouldn't mind dropping off an envelope with some money. They said they didn't, and here they were. They weren't practising Christians, but I told them the story about the gas bottle and that they were a miracle sent by God!

After they left, God spoke to my heart and said, 'Never ever say again that there is no way, because with Me there is always a way!'

Despite the draughty windows and uneven floors, I loved living in that flat and I enjoyed every minute of it. For me it was a place of refuge to come home to after visiting the flats, where I could relax and be at peace. I was tremendously grateful to Jesus for it and at the time I couldn't imagine ever living anywhere else.

Because the flat was in the middle of the red-light district it was ideally located for hospitality. For a couple of years I hosted a home group which one of the maids regularly attended. A couple of women used to visit frequently before starting their shift at a club, and a few women who worked in the flats would also come to see me.

Around that time I learned how to bake, and from time to time I would take freshly baked cakes to the women I visited. At Easter and Christmas we (the red–light team) would always take gifts to the flats. At Easter it was usually daffodils and a card or the *Why Jesus?* booklet, by Nicky Gumbel,[3] explaining how someone could find salvation in Jesus.

At Christmas I used to make different gifts. On one occasion I baked more than eighty ginger heart cookies with a delicious marzipan filling, and another time star-shaped cookies from a traditional Swiss Christmas recipe. One Christmas I bought about 100 small terracotta plant pots and filled them with scented wax to be used as candles. Although my kitchen was small, my living room was a good size, and for many weeks it looked like a

---

[3] London: Alpha International, 1991.

nursery till every pot was filled and made ready to take door to door.

The women who worked downstairs would, of course, hear the sounds of people coming and going but they never complained and on the whole, I had good relationships with everyone who worked there. Neither did they mind me popping in every other week or so.

One evening when I visited, the maid and the model were drinking cider. They asked me if I wanted to join them and I said yes, thinking that a bit of apple juice wouldn't do me any harm!

I used to work as a barmaid and hostess, and therefore knew the effect alcohol could have on people. I was no longer used to drinking alcohol, but I'd never had cider before, so I thought I'd give it a try. During our conversation I was sipping away on the cider, enjoying the sweetness of it. After I finished the can I could feel myself getting a bit light-headed, and I said it was time for me to go to bed. I left and went back upstairs.

I did manage the stairs, but when I was lying in my bed the room started to go round and round. I realised that cider was a drink to be reckoned with.

The next day the women commented with a smile that they had been thinking I wouldn't be able to manage a whole can of strong cider. They were quite amused by the little joke they had played on me!

The models downstairs would change from time to time and one of the young women I met was from an Asian background. She was very hardworking, serving clients many hours each day, sometimes even seven days a week.

She wanted to earn lots of money for her boyfriend who regularly came to pick it up.

It wasn't easy to hold a conversation with her. The only thing she seemed to be able to talk about with me was her boyfriend. She shared how much he loved and cared for her, and that one day they would get married and have a family. This was the dream of most of the girls I visited. They wanted to be loved and cared for, to marry their boyfriends and have a family. Unfortunately, it seldom happened.

One evening, in our church prayer meeting, our pastor suggested we should ask God for one person's salvation and to ask Him whom we should pray for. The first name that came to my mind was the girl from downstairs. I said to Jesus that I had probably misheard Him as I couldn't see her becoming a Christian. Whenever I visited I couldn't get a word in edgeways as she was totally obsessed with the boyfriend she was seeing. I therefore decided to play it safe and to pray as well for someone else who seemed more open and promising.

A few weeks later the girl's boyfriend overdosed and was hospitalised. She hadn't known he was taking drugs and was very distraught. Because of his condition he had a mental breakdown. During that time he had a vision of the cross of Jesus. On her next visit he said God had shown him that he was a sinner and that what he was doing was wrong. He told her he didn't want her to work as a prostitute any longer.

She didn't come back to the flat but took a job as a sales assistant. To cut a very long story short, a few months after that incident she experienced the love of Jesus and committed her life to Him. A few days later she had to move out of where she lived, but had nowhere else to go. I offered her to come and stay with me for a while, and she moved in the next day. She started to come to church and my pastor's wife, who was also from an Asian background, befriended her and helped her with some of the issues she was facing. She lived with me for about three months until she found a flat–share with some other girls from church, where she continued to grow in fellowship and following Jesus.

Her transformation really inspired me and, although she had many issues to face, as we all do, she persevered in her walk with Jesus. Today she is married with children and is leading a church with her husband, though not the same man as mentioned above.

7. Soho's Red-light District

Soho is still known for its red-light district, but thirty years ago it was seedier than it is now. The red-light district is only a very small part of Soho, which is located in the London Borough of Westminster with its famous architectural buildings, such as the Houses of Parliament, Westminster Cathedral and Buckingham Palace. Soho is in the heart of London and therefore has many cinemas, theatres, clubs, bars, cafés and restaurants. It's also a place for the fashion, music and film industry, and one of its famous streets is Carnaby Street where The Beatles used to shop!

Soho is also a residential area and still has its own primary school. Thirty years ago it had a local bakery and a butcher and an excellent vegetable and fruit market. Apart from the red-light flats it had sex shops and adult stores. There were also a couple of strip clubs and a few places called 'peep shows' where in badly lit cabins a half-dressed woman behind a window would expose some of her body for cash. Then there were clubs called 'clip joints', which I will talk about later.

There were men and women on the streets who were taking drugs and, of course, those who were selling them.

The drugs issue was usually well contained by the police, and if there were too many drug users they would be moved on. Using drugs is very costly, so many addicts would finance their habit by selling stolen goods in the red-light flats, the clubs and sometimes even on the streets.

There were women called 'clippers' who worked on the streets, of whom many were drug users. They would approach men and offer sexual services. The women would use various methods to get cash, but one of the more frequently used was to hand the man a key and send him to a certain flat. He would be told to enter the flat with the key and then wait for the girl who was supposed to join him soon after. The client was required to pay in advance, and of course the key never fitted the door, and the women always mysteriously disappeared.

A widely held misconception is that women who work in prostitution take drugs. This is only true for drug users who support their addiction by selling their bodies. Those whom I would call 'professional' prostitutes would not take drugs, and this was certainly true for the women I visited. In Soho a madam wouldn't hire a girl who was addicted to drugs, one of the reasons being that people who take drugs are often unreliable and untrustworthy. The expenses of a model working in a flat in Soho are quite high and therefore no business-minded madam would want to jeopardise her income.

During the first fifteen years of visiting the flats I went to approximately eighty-five flats in Soho and twelve in Mayfair. I went on regular door-to-door visits, sometimes with a co-worker but often by myself. Ideally I think it's good to visit in pairs. The reason why I often visited by myself was that I was full-time, whereas the people who volunteered had ordinary jobs and could usually visit only in the evening, once a week or sometimes only once a month.

The red-light team is always changing; some volunteers help out for one or two years while others stay for three or four. The co-worker with whom I worked longest is my friend and prayer partner Nicole. She served on the red-light team for ten years.

Two young women from YWAM did a year's placement and visited the flats with me. For several years I had students from a London–based Bible school, some of whom were involved in street evangelism, and others in visiting the women in the flats. I always had volunteers from various churches, including mine, City Gates Church.

I usually try to give everyone who wants to visit a chance to explore whether it is something God wants them to do, even if it's just for a short season. Many of the women who have been part of the red-light team and visited the flats have found that the experience helped them to step out of their comfort zone and to grow in trust and dependence on Jesus.

Building relationships with the women in the flats isn't easy. It often takes more than a year until someone is invited into an apartment. The team who visits usually has to get to know the women on their doorsteps first, before ever being invited in, and once a relationship is built up it can't just be passed on to someone else. We are working with real people and not just contacts! Therefore I've always made sure that I too have visited each flat so that none of the women is left by the wayside if a team member stops visiting.

The red-light team visits in pairs and they usually remain together until one of them moves on. It's not always easy to learn to work in pairs as each member has different strengths and weaknesses. Each team has their 'patch' and visits the same flats and, as they door-knock week after week, month after month, they will eventually get to know the maids and the models and build relationships.

As I have mentioned already, during the early years – and sometimes even now – the response would often be a voice behind a door shouting, 'We are busy,' or, 'We are not interested.' If we had five or six people open the door and talk to us that would be a good day. I door-knocked several times a week and so the women started to get used to seeing me. Then they began to open the door more readily.

As I'm rather an introvert, talking to people I don't know has always been a challenge. I don't have the natural ability to chat to people, and whenever I visit the flats I have to ask Jesus to help me with 'small talk', which I'm really not good at.

Of course, as I started to get to know the maids and models better, conversations became easier and more personal. Often before I leave a flat I ask if I can pray for them, there and then. On many occasions the women say yes and then I pray for the need they have just shared. If they had no specific prayer request, I would pray that they would experience more of God's love for them.

It often proved to be a challenge to focus on God's promise and to keep my eyes on Jesus rather than on the women shouting 'busy' from behind their doors. I sometimes thought that Soho wasn't the easiest patch, but on reflection I don't think there is actually such a thing as an 'easy' patch.

It must have been on a day when I was feeling particularly disheartened and discouraged that Jesus resorted to speaking to me through my aloe vera plant! I do not remember what it was all about, only that I ended up letting my frustration out on the poor plant. I actually spoke to it and said something like, 'You have been looking miserable for some time now and you're not producing any new shoots' – which was true – 'so tomorrow I'm going to bin you!'

The next morning when I got up I happened to glance at the aloe vera plant and, lo and behold, during the night it had grown six or seven new shoots! In that very instant Jesus spoke to my heart saying, 'Do not be deceived by appearances, by what you see with your natural eyes, because you don't know what I'm doing unseen!'

This experience had a profound impact on my heart and life. Jesus was teaching and challenging me in a visual and real way to 'walk by faith, not by sight'.[4]

Writing this, I'm still touched by His amazing grace: I'm glad and grateful that Jesus has more vision than I and that He sees the end from the beginning. If not, I myself should have ended up in the wheelie bin a long time ago.

The men visiting the flats have proved to be a different kind of challenge. I see men of all ages, businessmen,

---

[4] See 2 Corinthians 5:7, NKJV.

labourers, UK and foreign nationals, climbing the often narrow staircases to the flats. Some men who visit are driven by lust and instant gratification, while others are drawn by their curiosity or are lured into it by its seediness. Often, sadly, there are older men who are visiting a model who might be the same age as their own daughters or even granddaughters. Another sad truth is that some men are actually visiting out of loneliness. They're looking for a human touch as they feel lonely and isolated, starved of relationship in an often hostile world.

Sometimes men, clients seeking sex, would follow me. Seeing me coming out of the flats would encourage them to ask, 'How much?' A pleasant-looking businessman once caught me on a bad day, and when he asked that question I nearly jumped down his throat. Didn't he notice that my clothing wasn't typical of a model?

The Lord once sharply rebuked me for my attitude towards the men visiting the flats. I was walking down Berwick Street, feeling angry and upset about a client's manner towards one of the models, when Jesus stopped me, saying, 'I don't just love the women; I love the men too!' I knew this, of course, but I did find it hard to believe. But the men too were victims of Satan and needed to be rescued by Jesus. I personally didn't feel I should be the one witnessing to them, but at least I could be friendly and not judgemental.

I had to learn quickly, as I would often be sitting in a living room or kitchen with a maid when a client rang the doorbell. The maid would let him in and he would sit with us while waiting to be served. We would naturally try to involve him in our conversation, as we couldn't just let him sit there and ignore him. Sometimes the maid would introduce me as her friend from church, which some didn't find very amusing, but sometimes an interesting conversation would develop because of it. I remember one customer telling me his life story while waiting. He truly had a sad past, and I was able to tell him that Jesus would be able to give him a new life if he wanted one.

On very rare occasions, the model herself would ask me to pray for a customer. It is quite astonishing that Jesus doesn't seem to mind where prayers are prayed, as long as they are being prayed!

I also visited the 'clip joints', where women would try to entice men into their club and spend money by buying them drinks. Many of them offered some sort of entertainment, like pole dancing or striptease. They often had a bouncer or manager who would, by intimidation, extract as much money as possible from the clients. They would even accompany their customers to the nearest cashpoint to make sure they paid their bills, which could be several hundred pounds for a few drinks and hostess fees.

I myself worked in a seedy hostess club before I met Jesus, but it has always been a mystery to me how any of those clubs were allowed to function in the way they did. However, at the time of writing, they have all closed!

Those places were without scruple, and I remember some of the women who worked in them saying that it served the customers right to be ripped off. They came expecting pleasure and sex but walked out humiliated, having been exploited. I didn't say much, as I knew that my attitude would have been exactly the same before I was saved.

Jesus helped me to build many relationships in those clubs. I got on well with the women because I understood where they were coming from. I was able to relate to them, but also be a witness to the fact that Jesus could change someone's life, if that person wanted Him to.

I got to know some of the women very well, and as I lived in Soho I had the opportunity to invite them to my place for tea or dinner before they went to work. Two of them came on a regular basis, and I would cook for them and we would talk about God and the world. Neither of them committed their lives to Jesus during the years they worked in Soho, but Jesus taught me that if people wanted to be friends with me, then it wasn't just because of me but also because of who I was representing. During the time of our relationship, both women were able to taste and see that God is good, and I pray that one day they will remember and receive Jesus as their Saviour.

Even though I got on with many of the women, some of the club owners weren't keen on me. They didn't like me visiting the women, and one especially tried to intimidate me. I tried to avoid him as much as I could, but one day I hadn't been watching out for him. I didn't see him talking to his friend across the road when I stopped to talk to the girl on the door. She was interested in Jesus and was asking questions when he stormed across the road, shouting and swearing at me. He offloaded abuse on me and then went back to his friend.

At first I was quite shocked and shaken by the whole incident, but suddenly a righteous anger rose up within me. I crossed the road and stood in front of the man who had just verbally abused me and told him something to the effect that if he continued to oppose me talking to the women about Jesus, then God would judge him for it on the Day of Judgement. He was from Malta and a non-practising Catholic, and after this incident he never bothered me again.

As City Gates started to grow as a church and had more money coming in, the trustees agreed for the church to rent a small shop in Green's Court. By then we had another pastor as the first one had moved on. The shop was going to be used for various church activities and also as an office for our pastor, separated by a wall from the main room of the shop. One of his favourite activities at the time (and I believe it still is, although he is leading another church now) was witnessing to people about Jesus. Once or twice a week he would put a table in front of the shop window with books and tracts, and talk to whoever stopped and wanted to listen.

Now that we had a base I started to use it for the red-light prayer meetings and for the team meetings before the visits. There was a man at church who was witnessing to many homeless people and he started to use the shop in the evenings to give out sandwiches and hot drinks. The church started to open the shop on Friday evenings, with a table outside where we displayed literature, and we served hot drinks for anyone who wanted to come in and have a chat.

Apart from visiting the flats, the Friday evenings were something I really enjoyed. Most Fridays we were only a small group witnessing in Soho, but we had great times. Once I remember we had four young men who came in for a chat. They were soldiers, going off in a couple of days to serve abroad, and we were able to pray for them, asking Jesus to protect them. If it is not wonderful and amazing to witness and to pray for people, then I don't know what else is!

Soho is very varied and we had all sorts of people passing by; some of them were tourists, others businesspeople. We had the homeless and the drug addicts, there were men and women simply out looking for a good time, and of course there were the ones who were local and who either worked or lived in Soho.

8. God's Amazing Grace

One day my co-worker and I were heading to one of our more established contacts. I had known the woman for a number of years; we were about the same age and got on well. She had stopped working as a model and was working a few times a week as a maid.

Over the years she had told me a bit about her earlier life. She was Jewish, and in her younger years had been very beautiful. She fell in love with a man who became her pimp and who abused her shamefully. The scars on her body and face still bore witness to that terrible time in her life.

The flat she worked in was on two floors, and we were sitting as usual downstairs in the living room, chatting away. Suddenly I felt the presence of Jesus come into the room. It was so real that I looked behind me, thinking I would see Jesus standing there in physical form.

I was so surprised and stunned that I didn't know what to do. I didn't know if it was just me feeling it or if the others did too. After what felt like a very long silence I told my co-worker that we were leaving. I still felt utterly overwhelmed and helpless by His presence, unable to do or say anything.

Outside on the street I asked my co-worker if she had felt the presence of Jesus too, and she said she had.

A week or two later, when I wanted to visit that woman again, I was told that she wasn't working there any longer.

I had her phone number so I called her, and for the next few years we met from time to time. The experience I had had while visiting her in that flat somehow slipped my mind, but one day while we were having coffee I remembered and told her about it. I'll never forget what happened next. She looked at me and said, 'Yes, I know. Jesus came into the room, and that's the reason why I never went back to work!'

I have wondered about this many times since, and have asked the Lord why He doesn't do that more often. It would make work so much easier!

Many of the English models would start working as maids once they were over forty. This helped me because some of them were then more willing to invite me into their flats. They felt less exposed and vulnerable as they were now wearing more than just a bra and knickers. They were also usually better maids because, having worked as models themselves, they had a bit more compassion and understanding and were able to give the young models helpful advice about the job they were doing.

I've got to know three women from the north especially well. Two of them invited me on several occasions to visit them at home, where they introduced me to their husbands and children. All three of them started to work when they were young, and two of them were still married to the same man who had encouraged them to do so. That such a couple would stay together I have found to be quite rare.

When I first met them, two of them were already working as maids, while the other still worked as a model. This one told me years later how embarrassed and ashamed she used to feel when she had to go to the bedroom and serve a client while I sat with the maid and waited for her to finish. In spite of how she felt, she always invited me to come back. Her maid would very often cook dinner for the three of us and we would watch a film or just have a good chat.

When that particular brothel closed, the woman who worked as a model thought about doing something different with her life. The other two continued their jobs as maids and started to work in a flat nearby.

A few months afterwards, the one who had decided to stop working in Soho had an experience with Jesus. We, of course, had had many conversations about Jesus, and one day she decided to go to church near where she lived. The church wasn't 'charismatic', but the Holy Spirit didn't seem to mind, and fell on her anyway. She said that she had tried to get up but couldn't move, and it felt as if she were glued to her chair. She then experienced the love of Jesus washing over her, and she said that she had never, ever felt such love.

The pastor of the church was very understanding and helpful, and she continued going there. She did well for a while and followed Jesus very closely. She had a couple of serious addictions which troubled her, and she went for help and received counselling. She also started to attend a course which was designed to help her with the issues she was dealing with. Unfortunately, after a while she said that the pain was more then she could bear, and rather than pursuing the freedom which Jesus offered, she got involved in a relationship with another woman.

She left her husband and went to live with her new partner, but their relationship was violent and abusive, and things went from bad to worse. I still visited her occasionally and we kept in touch. The last time we spoke she said that she and her partner had separated. She is also now ill with several serious health issues. She still says that she'll never forget how much Jesus loves her. I pray that through His grace and His amazing, unconditional love, my friend's relationship with Jesus will be fully restored and that she too will be one of those women who on that day will be standing before His glorious throne, worshipping Him.

One of the women whom I got to know quite well worked in the basement flat I mentioned earlier. Unfortunately she moved on to work elsewhere as a model and I wasn't able to stay in touch, as I didn't have her phone number. This scenario happened often. I would start to get to know a model and then she would move on to work in another part of London or another city. That wasn't always easy to accept, as it seemed a bit of a waste of time to make all this effort to get to know someone and then they moved on. But of course it wasn't time wasted, as while I was getting to know the women, seeds of God's Word were being sown and some of His love and kindness displayed.

About three years had gone by when out of the blue this particular model called. She sounded very distraught and said that her best friend had been murdered at work, in another flat. Since I was the only Christian she knew, she asked if I wouldn't mind seeing her. A day or two later I went to visit her. We talked about the issues she was going through and, before I left, I prayed for her.

I don't like to lead people in what is called 'the sinner's prayer'. I prefer a person to take their time to think over whether they really want to make the decision to follow Jesus, rather than make a simply emotional commitment. As it has been said, 'The gift of salvation is free but not cheap!'[5]

Two days later I got another phone call from her saying that she had decided to give her life to Jesus, and that she wouldn't go back to work. That was good news! She lived on the outskirts of London and, as I wasn't able to follow up with her myself, I introduced her to one of our link churches. An added blessing was that a few months later her pastor called to invite me to help him baptise her.

Her journey with Jesus seemed to be plain sailing at first, but a couple of years later she came into a very stormy and dark season of her life. She left her church and cut herself off from every Christian she knew, including me. I didn't hear from her again until many years later when she recommitted her life to Jesus.

I had a good relationship with the woman who had negotiated for me and helped me to live in Great Windmill Street. I also knew her family and visited her often. She had recently started to come to our home group and began to learn more about Jesus. One day when I visited her at the flat she said she wanted to confess something, but felt

[5] Dietrich Bonhoeffer; also Rick Warren.

terribly embarrassed about it. She said very timidly that she was still shoplifting on nearly a daily basis. By then I had known her for several years and I was quite surprised that she'd never mentioned this before.

We talked about the situation and she said it had started many years before. At the time she was married and her husband was again in prison. She had three small children and very little money. In order to provide for them, she began to steal food and other things. Stealing became a habit, and even though she worked and was able to earn money to provide for her family, she continued stealing. She said she had tried time and time again to stop, but was unable to do so.

I said Jesus could help, and I prayed for her that He would help her to stop stealing. A couple of weeks later she said that my prayer wasn't working. I suggested that she pray herself, as I was sure Jesus had a solution to the problem. A week or so after that, we were sitting on the couch, talking, when suddenly she exclaimed, 'Oh, I forgot to tell you, I haven't nicked anything for a whole week!' That was, of course, very good news, and she was very happy that Jesus had answered her prayer.

After a few months she said she wanted to give her life to Jesus and be baptised. She knew by then that working in a brothel was wrong, but she had no other means of income. Her education was basic and her background challenging, and trusting God for one's livelihood doesn't happen overnight. I consulted my pastor about her being baptised and asked him to talk to her about it. I can't remember what my pastor said, but after discussing the situation with her, he decided that, despite her circumstances, we would baptise her.

Her baptism was a joyful event and I knew that in her heart she really wanted to follow Jesus. A couple of days later she went back to work as a maid, but we both knew things had to change. I told Jesus He needed to tell her Himself, as I didn't have the means to provide for her financially.

A few weeks later she told me Jesus had told her to stop working, and she had promised Him to stop before Christmas, which was just a couple of months away.

She gave in her notice and left Soho for good, as she had promised Jesus she would. A few days after she left her job an electrical fault occurred during the night when the building was empty, and it was gutted by flames. I'm not saying that God caused the fire, but nevertheless, it was a bit of a coincidence!

9. Lust is Not a Friend

Earlier, I shared how Jesus freed me from a long-standing relationship with Mark. Before this, I had tried several times not to go back, but each time I saw him I would be 'hooked' again. I would now define this kind of behaviour pattern as a demonically influenced emotional bondage or soul tie.[6]

After Jesus set me free, I did not miss or even think about Mark. Neither did I miss the sexual aspect, whereas before I became a believer I thought it would be impossible to live without a sexual relationship. I can honestly say that I felt totally fulfilled in Jesus; the emptiness in my heart was gone. It felt as if the relationship with Mark had never existed, and that I had a clean and new life ahead of me. The enemy, however, did not give up that easily and was very patient and cunning. Peter writes, 'Be alert and of sober mind. Your enemy the devil prowls around like a roaring lion looking for someone to devour' (1 Peter 5:8).

About five years went by, and in that time I only ever thought or spoke about Mark when I shared my testimony.

---

[6] A soul tie is a spiritual 'linking', often brought about through a sexual relationship. There can be unhealthy soul ties, but also healthy ones. For example, in the Bible, David and Jonathan had a healthy bond (see 1 Samuel 18:1).

I did not see him again, and even on my yearly vacations in Zürich I never bumped into him. Then one year, about a week before my holiday in Switzerland, I had a very graphic dream about the relationship I had had with Mark. I also felt in the dream that I needed to visit him urgently to tell him about Jesus, and that if I didn't he would be lost. The dream was repeated for several nights and, needless to say, I felt very disturbed by it.

I didn't believe the dream was from God as it was anything but edifying. I also concluded that if someone needed to witness to Mark, Jesus had enough people available to do so without getting me involved. I knew if I called him I would be playing with fire and would jeopardise the freedom I had found in Jesus. But the devil didn't give up, and for each of the following years, just before I went to Switzerland, I had similar dreams.

I believe when Jesus sets us free from any addiction we have to be very careful not to give into temptations. 1 Peter 5:9 teaches us to resist and stand firm in the faith, and another scripture says, 'Submit yourselves, then, to God. Resist the devil, and he will flee from you' (James 4:7).

After the dreams finally stopped, Satan didn't tempt me with Mark any more, but that doesn't mean he had stopped scheming, and the next time he set a trap he was more successful!

Since I became a Christian I have enjoyed being single and never wished to be married. I also never desired to have children of my own, even though I love them, and when other single women would speak about 'being broody' I had no idea what they were talking about. During the first ten years of my Christian life I met a couple of Christian men I felt attracted to, but I never seriously considered a relationship. I felt quite good about myself not needing a man, and I couldn't understand single women who were unhappy because they couldn't find a husband. I even knew a couple of women who started to go out with unbelievers, which I thought was wrong, and still do, and was very judgemental about it. I knew the proverb 'Pride goes before destruction, a haughty spirit before a fall' (Proverbs 16:18), but at the time I didn't realise that I had a haughty spirit and that I was proud and judgemental!

It wasn't that suddenly I no longer liked men, but Jesus filled that deep need in my heart where I so wanted to be loved and accepted. He also started to bring healing and restoration to my wounded soul, and at the time I would have said that I was 'sorted'; little did I know!

I felt happy and blessed when on my fortieth birthday I received some extra cash which enabled me to take a three-month, well-earned sabbatical in America. I love travelling and seeing different places, and on my way to Florida I had a stopover in Toronto, Canada, where I attended a conference on the Father heart of God.

In Florida I was joined by two friends and together we enjoyed visiting Disney World and the lovely beaches in Tampa. We also drove to Pensacola, where a revival was happening at the time. While queuing for several hours to get into the church building to attend the evening service, we happened to meet a couple from our church.

Once in the church building I was struck by God's holy presence. There was no worship group playing, just people mingling, but immediately I came under the conviction of the Holy Spirit and I realised that I wasn't as 'holy' as I thought I was.

I was able to stay in Pensacola for several weeks, though my two friends' holiday came to an end and they had to leave. After Pensacola I visited New Orleans, where I met up with friends from Switzerland who attended the Aglow International Conference. Everywhere I went I had a great time and my heart and mind were set on following Jesus, no matter what!

Two weeks before my sabbatical ended I wanted to stay one more week at a resort in Tampa, before visiting friends in Washington. While I was in Tampa something happened which I had thought would never happen to me: I met and fell head over heels in love with a man who, of course, wasn't a practising Christian! He was everything I would have looked and wished for in a man before I met Jesus. He was handsome, kind and rich, and at the time he was looking for a lasting relationship!

I remember an incident in which we were having dinner at a seaside restaurant in a beautiful romantic setting. He asked me about Jesus, what it all meant and how someone could become a Christian. Sharing the gospel with people was part of my 'job description', but at the time I was so enraptured by the whole setting that my mind went totally blank. I looked into his eyes and couldn't say a thing. I did have another couple of opportunities, which, fortunately, were a bit more successful.

My vacation came to an end and I returned to London feeling very lovesick. Although I knew the Word of God and what it taught about not entering a relationship with a non-believer,[7] I was still holding on to wishful thinking.

One night when I was lying in bed and thinking about what it would be like to be married to this man, I suddenly felt something crawling up my leg. It felt horrible and I shook it off, saying, 'Go away in Jesus' name!'

I knew it was an unclean spirit, but I had not learned my lesson. A week later I was thinking again of how it would be if ... and the thing that I couldn't see, but could certainly feel, crawled up my leg again. This time I repented, and told Jesus that I wouldn't lust any longer after a man I knew wasn't for me and I couldn't have. The unclean spirit immediately left and has never come back. By God's grace I don't think I have lusted after a man since, and Jesus has helped me, and is still helping me, to keep my heart and mind free from sexual sin.

This whole experience was very humbling, and since then I have more understanding and compassion for women who desire a husband. It also opened and exposed deeper issues in my heart which still needed healing. Where a few months earlier I had thought I was 'sorted', I realised that it would be a life's journey to be changed and become more like Jesus.

---

[7] See 2 Corinthians 6:14; 1 Corinthians 7:39.

PART THREE

2001-2010

10. A Strategic Word

When God showed me in 1988 that He wanted me to reach out to women in prostitution, it was a very vivid and memorable experience and I've never forgotten it. In fact, I often remind myself of that vision and pray into it. I thank Jesus that in the coming age I will see a multitude of women who have come out of prostitution and have received the gift of salvation and the robe of righteousness, standing in front of His glorious throne, worshipping Him.

Several years after that first experience, Jesus spoke to me again in a similar way. This time, too, the things I saw were very vivid and clear and I can still see them when I meditate and pray about them.

At the time I was at home in my flat and a colleague had stopped by, and it soon became clear that he wasn't in a very good mood. For some reason he started to discredit the work I was doing in Soho, and the last thing I remember him saying was something about people making too much fuss about the red-light district and that in truth nothing was really going on there.

He continued to talk, but his voice drifted away and Jesus started to speak to me. First I saw a map of Great Britain and a big tree covering it. Jesus said the tree represented prostitution and that its roots were in Soho. He said He was going to cut the tree down and that its fruit would fall off all over the nation. Then I became aware again of my colleague talking, and soon after, he left.

I understood the first part of the vision, but the second part, with the fruit falling off, I wasn't too sure about. I prayed about it for many months and asked Jesus to give me understanding.

As with the first experience, I didn't share it with anyone at the time. I think it's sometimes better to keep the things which Jesus gives us in our own heart for a while. Usually I start by meditating and praying about what I have been given, as I want to make sure His words become firmly rooted in my heart so that any negative words, or the devil's suggestion that I've dreamed it all up, cannot uproot the word or the vision I've received. Of course, everything should be tested first[8] and never allowed to contradict Scripture, which is the very Word of God.

At the start of each year I often go on a retreat, sometimes just for a week; sometimes longer. Around the start of the new century, I had a season of three years when God prompted me to take longer retreats, and these included long fasts. I used to fast on a regular basis, but to fast for more than seven days was quite a challenge. However, with God's help, it was manageable.

In January 2001 I fasted for twenty-nine days, and during that time I had the impression that Jesus was telling me I should pray for the flats in the red-light district of Soho to close. The scripture God gave me was from the book of Nahum, where He spoke about the overthrow of Nineveh (1:12-15). I had the impression that this also

---

[8] See 1 John 4:1.

confirmed what He had previously shown me through the vision of the tree. Before this, I might have occasionally prayed for the flats to close, but my logic always told me that the women would just move on to work somewhere else. But I firmly believed that Jesus had spoken to me through this particular scripture. The language was clear and strong, saying that although the enemy was there in full strength, nevertheless the Lord was going to cut him off. I often use the Word of God to pray, and so I started to pray those verses, even though at the time I couldn't really understand how it was ever going to happen.

From the Scriptures I understand that very often something has to break, shift or be removed in the spiritual realm before God's will or kingdom can be manifest in the natural. For me, one of the most vivid accounts is found in the book of Daniel, where we get a glimpse into the heavenly realms. There, an angel is speaking to Daniel, saying:

> 'Do not be afraid, Daniel. Since the first day that you set your mind to gain understanding and to humble yourself before God, your words were heard, and I have come in response to them. But the prince of the Persian kingdom [in this context, one of the fallen angels[9]] resisted me twenty-one days. Then Michael, one of the chief princes, came to help me, because I was detained there with the king of Persia. Now I have come to

---

[9] Fallen angels are believed to be the spiritual powers that were cast out of heaven with Satan. See Isaiah 14:12; Revelation 12:4-9.

explain to you what will happen to your people in the future, for the vision concerns a time yet to come.'
Daniel 10:12-14

Another well-known scripture on this subject is found in the letter to the Ephesian church where Paul writes, 'For our struggle is not against flesh and blood, but against the rulers, against the authorities, against the powers of this dark world and against the spiritual forces of evil in the heavenly realms' (6:12).

I believe the concepts of principalities and powers in the heavenly places are difficult for the Western mind to understand because we don't very often see demonic manifestations in our day-to-day lives.

To God's glory, I can testify that the first eight flats closed in 2003 when a property developer bought a whole cluster of buildings and turned them into a fashionable hotel. At the time of writing, in 2018, there are only twenty-three flats left.

After I started to pray more frequently for the red-light flats to close, some strange things happened to me, which I believe were from the enemy in response to my prayers. The following two things occurred during the same year.

One ordinary morning, when I woke up, everything seemed dark around me. There was something like a heavy and dark cloud or substance over me and I could hardly move. I certainly wasn't able to get out of bed, and the only thing I felt able to do was to ask Jesus to help me. I remember that after I asked Him to help I turned over in my bed and went back to sleep. Then a few hours later, around midday, I woke up and was completely fine. There was nothing wrong with me, and the only thing I could think was that if it should ever happen again I would just have to rebuke it and get out of bed.

It wasn't as easy as that, as it happened a number of times over several months, two or three times a week. If I woke up and the blackness was there it would feel so heavy that I felt unable to move. The only thing I could do was to ask Jesus, 'Please help me.' Then I would turn over in my bed and fall asleep again and wake up a few hours later feeling perfectly fine.

I talked to the church leadership team, of which I was a part at the time, and they prayed for me, but nothing seemed to help, until one day it just stopped and never came back.

The other occasion was, again, just an ordinary day, when I experienced a sudden weariness; it felt as if someone had opened a tap in my body and all my energy had flowed out. This too happened many times over a period of time, and it was bizarre, because wherever I was or whatever I was doing, I had to fight against dropping off to sleep. Even though I prayed and sought help, the situation prevailed.

One day I went to a conference where there was a speaker from France. The meeting was hosted by Susie and Ray Djan, who at the time were leading a church in Brixton, London. I didn't know them then, but I had the impression that I should go anyway.

During one of the meetings it happened again; it felt like a tap was opened in my body and all my energy flowed out like water. I was concentrating on not sliding off the chair when the speaker stopped his talk and looked at me.

He said he had been watching me and that he saw in the Spirit how my energy was flowing out of my body. He said he had asked the Lord if he could do anything for me, but Jesus had said He would deal with it in His own time and He would restore me.

I thought, 'Great! Thank you very much!' But at least I had some confirmation that I wasn't imagining it all.

Before the conference was over, Ray had a word of encouragement for me, and during a brief conversation he offered to be my mentor, which has proven to be a great blessing.

A few weeks later I noticed that I hadn't had any more episodes of loss of energy and that I was well again. As with the other experience, it had just stopped.

I believe that on both occasions it was a spiritual attack, but what I didn't understand was why I wasn't able to resist it or have authority over it. After all, Jesus did say that He has given us authority 'to overcome all the power of the enemy' (Luke 10:19). I still do not have an answer, but I'm at peace with the fact that Jesus knows. In the end Jesus did deliver me, and, as Scripture says, 'God is faithful; he will not let you be tempted beyond what you can bear. But when you are tempted, he will also provide a way out so that you can endure it' (1 Corinthians 10:13).

While writing this about praying for the flats to close, I have realised that those prayers had consequences for me. It could just have been a coincidence, but one year after Jesus gave me that scripture to pray in 2001, my landlord, who was eighty-three years old, decided to sell the property. He sold it to someone who assured him that it would be done up and used only for residential purposes.

The new landlord went back on his word and continued to rent out the flats below for prostitution. He also increased my rent far above my budget, and so unfortunately, at the end of July 2002, I had to move out.

I was naturally disappointed when I had to leave my home in Soho. I hadn't accumulated too much stuff; nevertheless, I had more than when I had moved in ten years earlier. I had two months to look for a new place, but besides Soho I was unable to decide where I wanted to live. I think I was still a bit shell-shocked by having to move.

A couple from one of the Ichthus churches offered me a place to stay while I looked for other accommodation, and I was very grateful. They lived in Plumstead, south-east London, and had just refurbished their basement. I can't recall the initial arrangement, but I ended up living there for a year, which was a great blessing.

Since August 2002 I haven't been able to live in Soho, which has been difficult for me to comprehend. I always believed the Lord would give me another flat in the area, but it hasn't yet happened. As I've previously mentioned, City Gates Church started to rent a small shop in Soho just around the corner from where I lived. After I moved house I was able to use the shop as my base, and I began to work from there, for which I'm grateful to God.

A few years later, Westminster Council closed the flats and the property was sold to developers. The house was pulled down and, along with some other properties, has given way to a hotel.

11. Prayer and Worship

I was sad to have lost my flat in Soho, but life goes on, and I continued to pray in our church centre in Soho for the flats in the red-light district to close. I also kept asking Jesus, 'What about the women? Aren't they just going to move on to another place? Isn't the red-light district just going to move somewhere else? Surely prostitution will not cease during this age?' I continued to ask the Lord about this because it seemed that either He wasn't answering or I wasn't hearing. I'm grateful that we have a God who is not a dictator, who is happy for us to ask questions, and to whom we can express our feelings, doubts and frustrations.

I still had questions about the second part of the vision concerning the tree and its fruit falling off. One day, actually while I was thinking about something else entirely, Jesus answered my question by reminding me of an incident in my own life.

As I recounted earlier, in my late twenties, while working at a private club in Zürich, one evening I stood as usual behind the bar watching what was going on, when suddenly I felt as though I was waking up from a deep sleep. I looked around me and thought that this wasn't a place where I should be working and that what I was doing there was wrong. I handed in my notice and left the club.

In hindsight, of course, I know it was God who had convicted me of sin, but at the time I had no idea.

Through that incident in my own life Jesus started to show me that through our prayers and the prayers of hundreds of other Christians unknown to me, the stronghold of prostitution over Soho would be weakened and eventually broken, and consequently a wake-up call would be released. Suddenly women will wake up and, like me, realise that what they are doing is wrong. They will wake up to the fact that they don't have to sell their bodies any more, that they don't have to be afraid of their pimp any longer, and they can be free and walk out of prostitution to do something wholesome and different if they want to.

This wake-up call won't be restricted to the women who work in Soho but, as the picture showed me, will extend to anywhere in this nation where God wants to move. I believe it is also relevant to all the women who have moved on or, for those from different nations, who now live back in their own country.

The following happened several years after Jesus spoke to me about 'waking up' the women, and it's a testimony to His faithfulness and the amazing work of the Holy Spirit.

I visited a maid, one of the Albanian women who previously worked as a model. The first time I saw her she was one of the most beautiful young women I've ever met and could have been a catwalk model. Unfortunately, she didn't know how attractive she was and her husband, a pimp, made sure it stayed that way. He talked down to her and didn't treat her very well.

We were talking, and she said that she had just recently returned from her holiday in Albania and that she had had something like a 'wake-up call' during her time away. She explained that one day, out of the blue, she felt as though she had just woken up and all of a sudden had seen her life with different eyes. She felt angry and ashamed as she realised how she'd allowed her husband to treat and take advantage of her. She said she received an inner strength to stand up to him, and that before this she'd never believed there was a God. However, this experience had been remarkable and had left her wondering.

She confronted her husband and told him she wasn't going to provide for him any longer; that if he wanted to be part of the family (by then they had three children), he would have to get a job and start supporting them. She told me that for the time being she would have to continue to work as a maid, but hopefully in the near future she would be able to find some other kind of work.

This whole incident was extraordinary and a great encouragement to me. Of course, she didn't know what Jesus had shown me and that He had said He was going to 'wake up' the women. I've never seen her since, but I heard that she eventually left her husband. My prayer is that one day, like me, she would not only wake up and change the direction of her life, but that she too would find salvation in Jesus!

Praying for the red-light district from within Soho, rather than Camden where I eventually lived, was important to me. When praying I prefer to be 'on the ground', so to speak. Our church shop in Soho was small and always very busy. I found it difficult to find space to pray, and I started to complain to Jesus about this.

I had recently read a book on night watches, *Reordering Your Day*, by Dr Chuck D Pierce.[10] I found the stories very inspiring and challenging, but that was as far as it went. I really like my sleep and I told Jesus that doing a night watch wasn't my thing.

I continued to complain that I hadn't enough space. Then one day Jesus interrupted me and asked why I didn't pray when no one was in the shop. I responded, a bit irritated by the question, that the only time the shop was empty was during the night. After what seemed a long silence I finally said, 'OK, Jesus, I'm willing to do a night watch.'

I did two night watches, each lasting twenty nights, the first one in January 2007, and then a second one later in the same year. When a year later I was preparing for a third, I realised that Jesus wasn't in it, and that that particular season for me to pray during the night had ended.

My first twenty nights were encouraging. I did some preparation and set aside some material which I wanted to study. The aim was to start at ten in the evening and finish around six in the morning without falling asleep. Jesus was helping me in this new adventure and it was exciting. He revealed fresh things to me through His Word, and new aspects of the spiritual realm. Jesus allowed me to have an encounter with an evil spirit, and this evil spirit challenged me about what I was going to do about his particular involvement in Soho. Jesus gave me wisdom and I

---

[10] Corinth, TX: Glory of Zion International Ministries, 2006.

answered that I wasn't going to do anything because He, Jesus, hadn't told me to do so. I later related the incident to my mentor and he said that often the enemy tries to wear us out by trying to engage us in a battle that Jesus hasn't called us to.

Ahead of my second twenty-day night watch I had great expectations. I was preparing for spiritual warfare and wanted a breakthrough, but I will never forget that first night! I started as planned, with worship and a bit of Bible study, and I could sense the presence of Jesus with me. Then I changed direction and started praising in a way that eventually should have led me into declaration and spiritual warfare. I persevered in this for about one hour, but when I realised there was no anointing I stopped and asked Jesus what was wrong.

His reply stunned me, and I could hardly believe what I'd heard. Jesus said He wanted me to stop and just sit with Him, as Mary had done.[11]

I protested and said, 'But Jesus, we're at war and I need a breakthrough. You can't seriously be telling me that You just want me to sit with You for eight hours a night for the next twenty days!'

He said, 'What you can't do in ten years I can do in a day!'

Well, that settled it, and reluctantly I changed my plans and started to study the Song of Solomon.

The following twenty nights weren't all spent just sitting at His feet: He knew in advance that I wasn't able to

---

[11] See Luke 10:39.

sit still for that long. But I had a wonderful time getting to know my soon-coming King of Glory just a little bit better.

I have always enjoyed worshipping Jesus in Soho, first in the flat I lived in and now in our church centre. I think it's the most amazing thing to be able to worship Jesus in the midst of a dark place, knowing that God inhabits the praises of His people[12] and that praising Him changes the spiritual atmosphere. The reason I worship, of course, is because God the Father and Jesus are worthy to be praised, but, at the same time, declaring His majesty, glory and power will put heavenly things into order.

Chapter 20 of the second book of Chronicles gives some insight into what can happen to the enemy when the people of God start trusting and praising Him, rather than looking at their circumstances. In this story, the land of Judah was surrounded by armies, and King Jehoshaphat proclaimed a fast for all the people. While they were praying and seeking the Lord, the Holy Spirit came on Jahaziel, the son of Zechariah, and he said:

> 'Listen, King Jehoshaphat and all who live in Judah and Jerusalem! This is what the LORD says to you: "Do not be afraid or discouraged because of this vast army. For the battle is not yours, but God's. Tomorrow march down against them. They will be climbing up by the Pass of Ziz, and you will find them at the end of the gorge in the Desert of Jeruel. You will not have to fight this battle. Take up your positions; stand firm and see the deliverance the LORD will give you, Judah

---

[12] See Psalm 22:3.

and Jerusalem. Do not be afraid; do not be discouraged. Go out to face them tomorrow, and the LORD will be with you."'
2 Chronicles 20:15-17

In verses 21 and 22, we then read:

After consulting the people, Jehoshaphat appointed men to sing to the LORD and to praise him for the splendour of his holiness as they went out at the head of the army, saying:
'Give thanks to the LORD,
for his love endures for ever.'
As they began to sing and praise, the LORD set ambushes against the men of Ammon and Moab and Mount Seir who were invading Judah, and they were defeated.

I believe we can learn a spiritual principle from this event. Paul tells us, 'For everything that was written in the past was written to teach us, so that through the endurance taught in the Scriptures and the encouragement they provide we might have hope' (Romans 15:4). To Timothy he writes, 'All Scripture is God-breathed and is useful for teaching, rebuking, correcting and training in righteousness' (2 Timothy 3:16).

I believe that praising God always has a spiritual significance, though that is not my primary motive for doing so. Nevertheless, I think it's important to remember these principles and to expect God to move on our behalf while we praise and worship Him.

One day while I was in Soho, I began my prayer time by singing to the Lord. The moment I started to praise Him,

Jesus gave me a brief glimpse into the spiritual realm and I saw strange-looking creatures running away. With their hands they were covering their ears, saying, 'Oh no, she is singing again!'

This incident showed me vividly how much unclean spirits hate worship of God. In the light of this I assume that angels love worship, and therefore would be joining us in our praises to the Lord. It is a beautiful thing to think that we can experience something of God's throne room here on earth as we simply worship and adore our awesome, great and all-powerful God!

12. Models

When I started to visit the women in Soho the majority of them were English, with the exception of some who were French and one who was German. The models who were a bit older and more established often had their own rented flat. They usually worked five days a week, had their own maid and would hire someone to stand in for them at weekends. The rest of the flats were run by madams who gave employment to the younger models. Although the model had to pay a fee for using the premises, they weren't as exploited then as they are today.

My experience has been that many of the English women I visited began to work in prostitution when they were young. Many of them had an abusive background and were therefore emotionally vulnerable. Often, but not always, they started because they met a man with whom they fell in love. He promised them true love and security, a family and children. He then skilfully manipulated them to earn money for him by working as a prostitute. To be wanted and loved is a natural desire, but unfortunately this desire is easily exploited.

Some women I knew worked for the same man for ten years or even longer. A break-up would usually happen either when he left for a younger model, or the woman herself decided that enough was enough. I have met a few women who worked for their partners or husbands for more than twenty years, to then be left not only with a broken heart and a destroyed life, but also financially broken, penniless!

The women I visited earned a good living and, on the surface, they appeared to be all right. They had no obvious physical need like someone who is homeless, a drug user or an alcoholic.

Trying to befriend the women sometimes proved to be a challenge. Many of them thought (as I used to) that working as a prostitute was just another job. Once when I knocked on a door the model, slightly irritated, asked me if I thought that she was more in need of saving than someone who worked in an office. Good question! My opinion is that the person in the office of course needs as much saving as she does; however, Jesus didn't tell me to knock on office doors, but on hers!

From time to time I have asked Jesus if there is a better or a different way I could reach out to and befriend the women He has called me to visit. Every time I have asked He has shown me the same picture of a pair of hands holding a heart, and He simply says, 'Go and show them My love!'

The French models I visited at that time had already been in Soho for many years and therefore were probably in their mid-thirties and forties. They usually worked in their own rented flats and employed their own maids who took care of the cleaning, cooking and opening the door to the clients. Some had settled in England whereas others had their permanent home in France. It took me many years to get to know them better, and still today (they are working now mainly as maids) there is only one who invites me into the flat for a cup of tea and a chat. The others are friendly and talk but our conversations always happen on their doorsteps. But who knows, maybe one day I'll get past their threshold!

The woman from Germany, I learned, came to England when she was in her early twenties. By the time I met her she was already around seventy and still working as a model. She worked in a small flat on the first floor of a three-storey building. One of her friends told me later that she owned the property.

I met her on one of my door-to-door visits and she immediately opened the door and invited me in. The small flat was crammed with stuff and not very clean. She asked me to sit down and made me a cup of tea. Instead of a maid she had an older man sitting with her to keep her company. The woman herself looked like my grandmother used to. Her grey hair was tied up in a bun and she wore a long, old-fashioned skirt. I couldn't believe that she still worked, and I doubted that anyone would stay after seeing how old she was.

I couldn't have been more wrong. After I had been talking to her for a while the doorbell rang and she went to answer it. When she came back into the room she asked me to leave, and on my way out she said I was welcome to visit her any time.

I visited her for several years, though not very often. It was the most difficult flat for me to visit and I found the whole situation repulsive. I asked her once why she was still working. She had enough money to stop. The house alone was worth a couple of million pounds at the time.

She said she wasn't able to stop, and that she had to keep on working. She once said she would work till the day she dropped dead.

Her life was heavily influenced, or even controlled, by unclean spirits. On a couple of occasions while I sat with her, talking, her voice suddenly changed and it was like someone else took over and spoke through her. Not only did her voice change, but also the topic of the conversation. Once, the voice started to proposition me, and that freaked me out a bit. Then the voice changed again and the old woman was back and talking again.

So I found it very difficult to visit and spend time with her. I didn't believe that she was too far gone to be helped, as Jesus has helped many people in her condition. Unfortunately, she wasn't seeking any help, and after a while I decided not to visit her any more. She knew where the church centre was and could see me any time she wanted.

A few years after I stopped visiting, a maid asked me if I knew that the old woman was losing her eyesight. I still passed her on the street from time to time, and she would be holding on to the arm of an older man whom I didn't know. I hadn't known she was going blind and she had never mentioned it. I went to visit her and asked her about it, but she said she was all right. The old man who was sitting with her said she wasn't, and told me she could no longer see. He said that during the last few years her eyesight had deteriorated and she was now blind. She was able to move around in the flat but the old man had to accompany her to go out. He stayed with her most days and looked after her, and yes, she still worked and had men seeing her for business.

I started to visit her again, but more for the sake of the older man as he started to ask me many questions about the Bible and Jesus. But a few months later he became very ill and died unexpectedly in hospital.

The old woman was now alone. Some of the older maids had tried to help her out, but despite her disability she was very strong-willed, difficult and ungrateful, and so they'd given up helping her. She had a sister who lived in England but she too had given up on her, and only visited her once or twice a year.

After the old man died I went to see her and asked how she was going to cope. She said she would manage and that she had found a woman who for an hourly wage would take her out four or five times a week.

I made some enquiries about the provision of some private help from an organisation for blind people. Every enquiry had to go through the NHS, but the old woman didn't want them to be involved. She was afraid they would rule that she wasn't able to live by herself and would put her in a care home. She didn't want to move and lose her home, and she still wanted to work. By then she was more than eighty years old and men were still seeing her for sexual services.

She asked if I would help her and take her to a restaurant for lunch and shopping a couple of times a week. I felt that Jesus wanted me to, at least for a while, and so I agreed to help her. She didn't know why she had become blind because she'd always refused to see an eye specialist. I asked her why and her answer was that she had been afraid to be told she was going to lose her sight! Now she was blind and had nothing to lose, so we went to see a specialist in Harley Street.

After the doctor examined her he asked why she hadn't come before. She had glaucoma and it could have been treated if she had come for help sooner. She wasn't someone who showed her emotions and she never talked about it, but I wondered how she felt after she found out that she could have been helped had she not listened to her fears. Satan is a hard taskmaster!

I took her shopping and to the restaurant a couple of times a week for more than two years. She allowed me to pray for her a couple of times, but that was all. The last time I visited her was before one of my summer holidays to Switzerland. Before I left I told her that Jesus still loved her and was able and willing to help her. The only thing she had to do was ask Him. She listened but didn't say anything, and I left.

When I came back from my holiday I called her but she said she didn't want to see me any more. Someone told me she had a new man who was taking her out. Two years later she died of pneumonia in hospital.

That woman's life was the saddest I've ever seen, but I know that even she could have called out to Jesus and He would have saved her. And, of course, only Jesus knows if she recalled my words and reached out to Him in her last hour of need.

During all the years in Soho the above incidents were the only ones where I encountered such demonic activity while visiting someone. I would have liked to help this woman because I know that Jesus had the power to set her free. But I believe that someone can only be helped if they want to be, and unfortunately she never responded to my invitation.

My experience of praying for deliverance from unclean spirits has been mainly through the prayers and ministry I've received for my personal freedom. I have had a couple of opportunities to pray for people, but my knowledge of the subject is limited. The Gospels recount many incidents in which Jesus casts out evil spirits. I believe that even today many Christians could benefit from such prayers, as unhealthy or ungodly behaviour patterns could be the direct result of an unclean spirit. In my personal life and ministry, two books on the subject, which I have found helpful and enlightening, are *They Shall Expel Demons* and *Blessing or Curse: You Can Choose*, both by Derek Prince.[13]

It all happened very gradually, but after I had been working in Soho for about ten years, young women began to come to work here from Russia and nearly every country in Eastern Europe. Today, at the time of writing, I can only think of two or three English models still working in Soho.

One of the first of these women I met spoke a little English. She was very upset, and told me that she was from Russia. She said she had known before she came that she would be selling her body, but the organisation she came with had deceived her. They had told her she would be working as an escort having only one or two clients a day, and that she would be free to go out whenever she wanted and enjoy her life.

---

[13] Hitchin, UK: Derek Prince Ministries, 1998; Ada, MI: Chosen Books, 1998.

As it turned out, she found herself in a brothel in Soho, working a fourteen-hour shift, serving thirty or more clients a day. She was told she owed the organisation £30,000 and that she had to pay it off as quickly as possible. She was financially exploited not only by the people who brought her into the country, but also by the madam who ran the brothel. In addition to the debt she had to pay off, she was charged several hundred pounds rent a day for using the premises she worked in. To leave the country wasn't an option for her as the organisation had her details and wanted their money.

I don't know if all the women who came through that particular organisation knew they were going to be working as prostitutes. What they experienced was bad enough, but can you imagine if some had thought they were going to be working as waitresses or cleaners?

There wasn't much we could do to help other than pray. Many of the women could only speak a bit of English and it was difficult to communicate. They also didn't want to get involved with the police but wanted to pay off their debts as quickly as possible and then work for themselves.

We prayed for several years, then one day we read in the newspaper that the woman who was part of that particular organisation and 'looked after' the women in London had been caught and sentenced.

Many women started to come from the Czech Republic, Poland, Ukraine, Moldova, Bulgaria, Estonia, Latvia, Slovenia, Hungary, Slovakia and Croatia. However, the majority of the women I met came from Lithuania, then Albania and during the last ten years mainly from Romania. Some came with the help of an agency or organisation. Others came illegally and were often accompanied by a boyfriend.

In order not to be too overwhelmed by the new situation, I had to learn to focus on Jesus rather than the circumstances. It was also difficult to communicate as the majority of the women had to learn English first. We ordered literature in each of their languages so that when we visited we could at least give them something to read.

I don't know all the details, but it appears that many of the Lithuanian women came via an organisation disguised as a job agency. In their home country they responded to an advert offering employment in England. The people who then interviewed them promised them a job with accommodation. In exchange they had to pay an agency fee, an amount of money which seemed reasonable and which could be paid off gradually over time.

One of the women I talked to was from Lithuania and in her mid-thirties. She said she was a chef and had responded to an advert in her local newspaper. She went for an interview and accepted the job, hoping to gain some new experience while working abroad. She arrived at a London airport where she was picked up by a woman, her new employer. The woman then drove her to her accommodation and asked for her passport. The next day she was brought to Soho where she was told to work as a prostitute to pay off the money she owed the agency. By the time I met her she had already been working for a few months. She told me in broken English that she had met a man, a client, who was going to help her leave. A few days later she was gone.

In fact, several of the Lithuanian women I've met left with a client or returned to their country. It seemed that that particular organisation didn't have the manpower to follow them up.

Many of the maids were kind to these young women. I know of some who helped the models to save money. Many of the models were searched when they got home from work: the person who 'looked after' them wanted to make sure they weren't hiding any money. The maids would keep some of their earnings each day until they had saved up enough money to pay for a flight home. The organisations could no longer keep the women's passports, as the vice squad started to want to see their documents when they visited the flats, and this made it a little easier for those who wanted to escape.

Many of the young Albanian women were friendly and willing to engage in conversation. Some were open to talking about Jesus and some asked regularly to be prayed for. When their boyfriends first brought them to Soho they were on average eighteen years old and a very few were in their mid-twenties. Only gradually would they start to talk about their families and why they had come to England. Their stories were all similar: they had met a man who had promised them the world, and then found out too late what it was all about. But even now, working in Soho in a brothel, they still believed themselves to be in love. They believed that they would work for only a few years till they had saved up enough money, and would then start a family with the man they loved.

I knew that telling the young women that their boyfriends were just using and exploiting them would be useless and counterproductive. The outcome would be that they would go and tell their boyfriend. He, of course, would deny it and assure them of his undying love and forbid them to talk to me any more. I wanted to be able to continue seeing them and to build up a relationship so that one day, when they were confronted with the truth, they could talk to me if they wanted to.

A couple of maids lost their jobs over such conversations with the models, as some of the madams had financial arrangements with the Albanian pimps. They didn't want to lose a model, as they did very well for themselves. Some of them tried to excuse their corrupt behaviour by saying it was the girls' fault and that if they weren't so stupid they wouldn't work for a man in the first place.

One of the young Albanian models I met was particularly friendly and introduced me to a friend of hers who worked in a flat nearby. Her friend, who wasn't very well and was scheduled for an operation, asked for prayer.

A few months later the girl's friend returned to Soho. Her health didn't allow her to work as a model and she started to fill in as a maid instead. Eventually the two of them were able to work in the same flat, which they were very happy about. I usually visited them once a week. Sometimes they cooked dinner and we ate together, watched their favourite soap, and chatted. They were very open to Jesus and we had many conversations about Him and prayed nearly every time we met.

On occasion, one of the model's regular customers would join us. He had his own business, was divorced and felt lonely. He said he didn't want to go out to pick up a woman for sex and that therefore this arrangement suited him. At first he didn't want to stay while I was there, but the model assured him that I wasn't going to judge him. Over the course of time I got to know him a bit better. Of course, I didn't agree with what he was doing, but at the same time he wasn't going to be able to change without meeting Jesus first. I pray that one day he will have a personal encounter with Jesus and be saved.

One year, before Christmas, I felt very tired and was looking forward to a break and some time off. I often spent Christmas with my family in Switzerland but that year I had decided to spend Christmas by myself in my flat in Camden. I loved living there and if I did get bored I could always visit people from my church who lived in the area.

The two women knew I had nothing planned for Christmas and that I just wanted to stay at home and 'chill'. But despite this they wouldn't take no for an answer and tried for weeks to persuade me to spend Christmas Day with them.

The madam decided she wanted rent money for the 25th, and so they had to work! Although I was very fond of them both, the last thing I wanted was to spend Christmas Day in a brothel. But in the end, a few days before Christmas I gave in and promised that I would come.

Before they came to England they had never celebrated Christmas because Albania had been a communist country. One of the women said that her grandmother used to go to church and believed in God, and that she too believed in God and knew that Christmas was about celebrating the birth of Jesus. And so this is what they wanted to do, celebrate the birth of Jesus, and both were looking forward to it like little children.

When I arrived on the 25th there was a lot of activity in the tiny kitchen as both girls were busy preparing traditional Albanian dishes. Work, of course, didn't stop for Christmas and so when the doorbell rang the model had to leave the kitchen and serve her customer. They had also invited a regular client who was originally from Turkey and from a Muslim background. There wasn't much room in the kitchen, but we managed to cram in four chairs so that we could all sit down and eat. The food was delicious and we enjoyed eating while listening to carols on the radio or television.

After the meal, one of the women asked if I would pray and if I would also pray for her customer, who had family difficulties. I explained to the man that I would pray to Jesus and in His name. He said this was all right with him and the four of us joined hands and I prayed. As I was praying, the presence of Jesus came very gently into the room and the woman who had asked if we could pray called out, full of excitement, saying, 'Can you feel the presence of Jesus, can you feel His presence?'

We all felt His wonderful presence and once more I was deeply touched by His amazing grace. Jesus really cares about people and nothing escapes Him. He heard the prayers of four people, praying in a tiny kitchen on the first floor of a brothel in Soho, and decided to visit us by His Holy Spirit.

After a couple of years, and another serious life-threatening incident, the maid stopped working. She received Jesus as her Saviour and since then has been faithful in following Him. Another few years later, and after much hardship and a broken heart, the other girl too finally stopped and is now working in a normal job. She had to work very hard to get where she is now and she knows and acknowledges that Jesus helped her. She hasn't given her life to Jesus yet, but I pray that one day she will. We're still in touch, and on sunny days and long summer evenings the three of us love going to Regent's Park for a picnic or just a long stroll.

13. Maids and Madams

Many of the maids are friendly, ordinary housewives, mothers or even grandmothers. A job like this obviously isn't advertised in the newspapers; one usually gets to work in a flat through a friend or a relative. For us who visit, it's very important to have a good relationship with the maid as she's the one who usually opens the door. If she doesn't like or trust us, we'll never get past the threshold to speak to any of the models.

In some flats there are two generations working because some maids encourage their daughters to work. This is very sad because once they're in the job it's very difficult to get out. This work brings with it a spiritual impact and bondage, which of course the women are unaware of.

During my early years in Soho I met four women who turned out to be sisters. Two of them still work in the flat I'm writing about. One of the sisters told me that one of them used to work as a model, but all the others had had normal jobs. For one reason or another all three of them had eventually given up their regular jobs to work as maids in one of the brothels in Soho.

One of the maids had two daughters, the younger of whom also worked as a maid. I got to know her well and visited her most weeks. We had many conversations about Jesus and she asked me on several occasions to pray for her. Eventually, after visiting her for several years, she decided to give up her job as a maid and to move on with her life. The other daughter, the elder one, had always refused to work as a maid. She told her mother that what she was doing was wrong and that she would never get involved with it.

A few months before the younger daughter left her job as a maid, the older one did an Alpha course. She had a neighbour who was a Christian and had been witnessing to her. She invited her to the course and she agreed to go. My co-worker and I were very happy about this as we had been praying not just for the maid, but also for the family, for many years.

A few months later the mother told me that her daughter had attended the whole Alpha course but had decided not to commit her life to Jesus. The bizarre thing is that after rejecting the offer of Jesus' salvation she accepted the offer from her mother to work in the brothel as a maid, something which she had previously absolutely despised! Sadly, she's also one of the maids who, up to the time of writing, have never invited me or any of my team into the flat to talk to the models. The reason she gave me once was that the models weren't interested in Jesus anyway, so there was no point in me coming in!

Her mother and aunt, though, are still inviting me in to have a chat and to talk to the models. The two of them believe in God and pray on a regular basis. They've asked me on several occasions to pray for them and their families. I've explained the gospel to both of them many times, telling them that Jesus is the only person who could forgive their sins and save them, but somehow they seem unable to grasp this simple truth. Only once, when I discussed the subject of why Jesus died for us on the cross, did one of them have a brief moment of revelation. It was like Jesus took away the veil and she suddenly said, 'You mean that if I don't receive Jesus as my Saviour I'll be lost?' I said, 'Yes,' but unfortunately she didn't respond.

One of the madams whose flat I visited regularly used to try to convince me that what she was doing was all right. She completely ignored the fact that she was supplying jobs for young women who worked for a pimp. She said they all wanted to work and did so of their own free will. Many of the women might not have been physically forced or beaten up to do so, but I'm sure none of them just woke up one morning and said to themselves, 'Today I'm going to start working as a prostitute!'

The madam was from a Catholic background and believed that because she had been baptised she was going to be saved. She said that for the time being she wasn't going to confession as she would come back to work the next day anyway. She said she loved money and wasn't willing to give up the brothels – she had several of them. She said she would have enough time to repent on her deathbed. I replied that she might not have time to repent before she died, and she then gave me one of her looks which meant that she no longer wanted to talk about the subject.

Even though after this her attitude towards me wasn't particularly friendly, she still allowed me into her flats to visit the maids and models. One day when I was visiting with a co-worker, she opened the door and asked if we could pray for her grandson who was critically ill in hospital. We said we would, and the next week when we went to see her she said her grandson was out of danger and she thanked us for praying. By now she must be well over seventy years old and is still working and running a couple of brothels. Some of her flats have been shut down during the last few years but she is still hanging on to the ones she has left.

I'm grateful that not all madams have an attitude like this. I used to visit a former model who had started to run her own flat. She had a young woman from Eastern Europe working at her place. Sometime later when it was the model's birthday they went out for a drink to celebrate. The young model started to open up and share about her life. She told the madam that her father had sold her to two men who then forced her to work in prostitution. The madam was so shocked by her story that she took the girl home to live with her and her family. When the two men came looking for her, the madam told them she hadn't come back to work and that she didn't know where she had gone.

14. Practising Hospitality

At the same time as moving house (from Soho to Plumstead), I was getting to know one of the young Albanian models better. She was going through a difficult time and, like many of the other young women, she had fallen in love with a man who had turned out to be a pimp. Such men are great manipulators, and they know exactly what a young girl wants to hear. With smooth words and empty promises they trap a vulnerable woman before exploiting her.

After working for that man for several years, she happened to find out he had another woman in Albania. She was very upset and hurt, and wanted to leave him. She asked if I could help her and whether she could come and stay with me. She wasn't able to leave England straight away as her documents were with the Home Office.

I no longer had my own place, but I talked to the family and they agreed that she could come and stay with us till she got her papers. Taking someone in is always a bit of a risk. Women who have a pimp are like people who are on drugs. Often they are unable to think for themselves as they are so intoxicated by the relationship and the man they work for. They also suffer something like withdrawal symptoms, and the urge to go back to the man they have just left can become so overwhelming that, no matter what he's done, they want to return to him.

Knowing her situation, I had my doubts, but she was adamant that she wanted to leave her pimp and go back to her family. She came and lived with us, and on the first Sunday she asked if she could come to church with me. She enjoyed the service and said she really wanted to change and have a new life. She said she didn't want to work as a prostitute any longer and wanted to turn away from it all. I remember, and I'll never forget, that while she was saying these things her countenance altered. It was as if a light was being turned on inside her, and her eyes became brighter and her appearance changed. It was remarkable, and I was quite overwhelmed. But although she experienced something from God, she wasn't in a place where she fully wanted to turn her life over to Jesus.

The bondage and addiction to the man she used to work for was strong and she could talk of nothing else but him. The only reason she didn't run back to him was because he happened to be back in Albania for a few months. While she was waiting for her documents, we offered to pay for her to go to school to improve her English. We thought the change would help her to get her mind off her situation, and that at the same time she could meet some other people. The only friends she had worked in Soho, and visiting them didn't help. One of the maids was trying to persuade her to come back to work. She said she was silly to go back home without money and that now she was rid of her pimp she should work for herself.

After she had lived with us for three weeks she came back one evening from visiting her friends in Soho. I immediately noticed the change: the light within her had gone and she looked like her old self again. She said she had decided to go back to work and make some money for herself before returning to her family in Albania. A couple of days later I helped her with her bags and we dropped them off with a maid in Soho with whom she was going to stay for a while. She didn't keep in touch but after a few months I heard that she was back with her boyfriend.

Today she's still working for the woman who persuaded her to make some money for herself. She hasn't spoken to me since, but I wonder if she's ever thought about how her life could have turned out had she not listened to the voice of that woman.

As I mentioned earlier, apart from visiting the flats, I also helped with an outreach on Friday evenings. One Friday two people from the church came to our shop accompanied by a young woman who seemed frightened. They said that they had found the woman sitting on her suitcase in the middle of Leicester Square. She looked lost and distraught, and they thought we might be able to help.

We couldn't just leave her on the streets. She could hardly speak English and did indeed look scared and traumatised. I thought we could take her in for the night and try to find out the following day what had happened to her and how we might help. At the time, before I moved into my own accommodation in Camden, I shared a flat with two other women near Camden Town. I called my flatmates and explained the situation and they agreed that I could bring her home for the night.

The next day we tried to have a conversation with her. Her English was very poor but we managed to find out that she was Jewish and had been brought up in Russia. She had recently moved to Israel where she hadn't been very happy. Through the internet she had got to know a man in London who had invited her to come and live with him. We got the impression that she thought he was going to marry her, and so she had packed all her things and come to London. What had happened next she didn't say in detail, only that he had given her a pair of knickers and a bra, and that was when she had left him. I assume he had wanted her to work as a prostitute and, thanks to God, she had been able to leave before it was too late.

She didn't know where to go and had ended up sitting on her suitcase in Leicester Square. For one reason or another she also had no money and couldn't return to Israel. One of my flatmates offered to pay for her flight, but she said that she would like to find a job and stay in London for a while. I was about to go on holiday to visit my family in Switzerland. My flatmates decided they would put her up for one month. They said that if she couldn't find a job within a month she would have to go back to Israel, and she agreed.

When I came back from Switzerland after three weeks the young woman was still living there. She hadn't been able to find work, and decided as promised that she would go back to Israel. My flatmate booked her a ticket and said it was a gift. The woman insisted she would reimburse her once she was back home. Sure enough, a few months later my flatmate received a transfer reimbursing her for the flight.

One day when I was visiting I became very concerned about a model from Lithuania. I met her in a flat where I knew the maid well. She looked like she had been crying and was very upset and appeared frightened. I asked the maid about her and she said that she didn't know her. The only thing she knew was that the girl was from Lithuania and new to the job. I tried to speak to her but she couldn't speak English and I wasn't able to ask her any questions.

During the night I couldn't sleep and I couldn't get that girl out of my head. I knew something was very wrong and I asked Jesus to help me find out more about her. The next day one of the maids called me to ask if I could come to see her. I went, and to my surprise the Lithuanian girl from the previous day was there too. The maid said she was worried about her, that it was obvious she didn't want to work, and wondered if I could help. I tried again to talk to her but it was impossible to have a conversation. We couldn't ask one of the other Lithuanian girls to interpret because that could have put them both at risk. I said I was going home to think about it and to try to find someone who could speak Lithuanian.

I went home and asked Jesus about it. I suddenly remembered that I had met a man from Lithuania some time ago who worked with another church. I knew the pastor of that church and phoned him. I explained the situation and said I needed to speak to this man urgently. The pastor said that the man I was looking for just happened to be there. I knew this was no coincidence and that Jesus was working something out. I spoke to the man and he was willing to talk to the girl. We exchanged phone numbers and I said I would call him as soon as I got back to the flat where she worked. She could then talk to him and explain her situation.

I went back and told the maid I had found someone who could speak the model's language. I called the man and they talked. She explained that she had been brought to England under false pretences. I realised then that she had come with the same organisation as the woman who had thought she was going to work as a chef. The Lithuanian man offered to call the police on her behalf. She said she was scared and didn't want the police involved. He was a married man with children and so he offered to take her home to be with his family till she knew what she wanted to do. Again she said that she was too scared to leave, but in the end he was able to persuade her.

Had she not been so traumatised by her situation she could simply have got dressed and left. None of the maids would stop a model walking out if she didn't want to work.

In order to get her out of the flat we planned an escape. We arranged that the next day the Lithuanian man I had called would come to the flat pretending to be a client. She would be working in a different flat, which was helpful, as I didn't want the maid who helped us to be blamed for her disappearance. The only problem was that we didn't yet know which flat. So the next day we waited till the maid found out where she was working. Once we knew, the Lithuanian man went to the flat and pretended to be a client. He went into the bedroom, where she was waiting for him. They left by a different door which led to the staircase of the building, and despite the cameras the maid didn't see them leaving.

The Lithuanian man took the girl home to his family, where she stayed for nearly a year. She started to go to church with them and a few months later gave her life to Jesus. One thing which I have to mention is that there were only two or three flats in Soho where the bedroom had a second door leading straight into the staircase. Jesus is amazing and His plans are truly perfect!

During one of my visits I met a young woman from Poland. She was very unhappy at the time and wanted to have a chat. She had come to London to learn English and had worked as an au pair for a family on the outskirts of London. Sometimes in the evenings she would meet with other au pair girls in the local pub. This hanging out together caught the attention of some Albanian men who then tried to befriend them. She subsequently fell in love with one of the men, and after a brief time of knowing him she left her job and moved in with him.

He shared a flat with another man whose girlfriend worked as a prostitute. She said that her boyfriend didn't force her to work but encouraged her to do so from time to time. After she had lived with him for a few months she eventually gave in and started to work in a flat. I asked her why she hadn't left when she still could, and gone back to Poland. She said she was in love with him and didn't want to go back home, and that she had had an unhappy childhood, her father being an alcoholic.

When I met her she had already been working for a couple of years. The reason she was unhappy wasn't because of her job, as she said she didn't mind working for her boyfriend. She was upset because he had recently told her he was married to someone in Albania, and that he wanted to bring his wife to England. He told her she was the only one he really loved and cared about and they could still be together, as he would come and see her every day.

This scenario sounds like one from a second-rate film, but this really happens and girls continue to work for men like this because it's less painful to believe his story than to face the fact that he is a liar and that she has been shamefully betrayed and used.

She told me she wanted to leave him but didn't have any money to do so. Most of the money she earned she gave to him or used to buy him expensive clothes. I invited her to come and stay with me for two or three months. She could live rent-free and save up for a deposit and her first rent. I knew she would still be working and planned to continue to do so, at least for a while. The only condition I set was that she must not answer his calls nor ring him. I knew this was going to be hard for her, but she said she wanted to leave him and therefore wouldn't get in touch.

He was away for a couple of days and she left his place and came to live with me at my one-bedroom flat in Delancey Street, Camden Town. She was all right for the first two days but then started to miss him. During the first week I think she didn't call him. He eventually rang her, and of course she answered. As they talked she realised that he hadn't yet noticed she had left. He was with friends and hadn't gone to see her. He persuaded her to meet him so they could talk things over.

She said she would come back in a few hours and that she would call me. I didn't hear from her for twenty-four hours and her phone was switched off. I was very worried about her because you never know what such men might do. Usually they don't just let a girl walk out on them. They earn a lot of money from a model and to lose one would mean losing income.

When she finally came back she said they had spent time together and that she had turned her phone off because she didn't want him to know she was staying with me. I was very upset and angry and wanted to give her a piece of my mind, but Jesus suddenly stopped me. He interrupted my thoughts and reminded me of my past and how I used to behave when I was her age, and asked me why I expected her to behave differently.

My anger subsided and she continued to stay with me until she had enough money to rent her own place. She was honest, saying she would continue to see him and that she didn't want to break if off yet. When she left she said I was the only one who had ever helped her without demanding anything in return. Through me I hope she met the kindness of Jesus and that one day she will meet Him personally and get to know Him as her Saviour.

PART FOUR

2011-2018

15. The Sower Sows the Seed

Very early on in my walk with Jesus, during a time of meditation, He gave me a picture of a dandelion. I had the impression that He was saying I was going to be like this flower. I wasn't very pleased about this as I didn't think dandelions were pretty, and what is more, I used to collect their leaves to feed my sister's guinea pig. I told Jesus I would rather be a rose than such an ordinary flower! Then Jesus reminded me that at the end of its season the dandelion turns into a silver ball with hundreds of little seeds, and that when the wind blows over it all those little seeds are dispersed. That didn't sound so bad after all, and I concluded that it would be a good thing to be like a dandelion. It would be great to be enabled to sow God's seed, His word, into lots of people's lives, and this I have been doing ever since!

My work consists mainly of sowing God's seeds. Usually several times a week I go, either accompanied by a team member or by myself, and knock on the women's doors in Soho or Mayfair. The women I visit aren't usually ready to hear God's word straight away and many think of God only as a judge. Especially in this type of work, many women feel guilty about what they are doing, without necessarily showing or admitting it. I know it's not easy for them to open the door to us and I do understand if they are reluctant to do so. Once they get to know us a bit they realise that we haven't come to judge, and often they become more relaxed and eventually invite us in.

For me, sowing God's word is not just talking about how someone can receive salvation, but also showing God's goodness by being kind, caring and loving towards the women we meet. The Scripture says that 'God's kindness is intended to lead [people] to repentance' (Romans 2:4). When I first started, there were too many flats to take regular gifts to. For the last few years, since the majority of the flats have closed, every team takes a small gift when they visit door to door. They usually take roses or chocolates or, more recently, fruit, as some of the women always say they are on a diet. One of my former team members always baked the day before she visited: delicious but healthy cookies made with oats, raisins and honey. I usually wrap colourful sweets or toffees in cellophane with a small ribbon and a label telling them that Jesus loves them, that they are precious, or that God's love is kind. One of the maids once told me she takes the sweet home to her child to remind her that Jesus loves her!

Every person is individual and therefore needs something different from God. Before we visit the flats we always ask the Holy Spirit to help us to be sensitive to His leading so that He can direct our conversations. The words we say are important; the book of Proverbs says, 'Gracious words are a honeycomb, sweet to the soul and healing to the bones' (16:24). Many women have hard hearts because of their life experiences, and they often blame God for these. Therefore, we're always praying and asking God to soften the women's hearts by His Holy Spirit so that when we share His words of hope and encouragement they will be able to receive them. We read in Isaiah 55 that God's promise is that His word will not return to Him empty, but that it will accomplish His desire and achieve the purpose for which He sent it (verses 10-11).

During the first ten years when I visited the flats, the women would often ask me how I became a Christian. The English models especially were intrigued and asked questions. When the women started to come from abroad, communication became a bit more difficult and I had to order relevant literature in all their different languages. Unfortunately, once they learned English they rarely asked about my faith and so I decided to write my testimony to give to them.

I think people in general like to read about other people's lives, and many women have now read my story. This is all good seed sown into the lives and hearts of the women, many of whom have experienced rejection and therefore have wounded hearts. My prayer is that through my story many women will find hope in Jesus, and in His timing be able to receive the salvation of their souls through His healing love.

I haven't always found it easy to be a 'sower', and on more than one occasion I have complained to Jesus about this. I haven't got much to show for all my sowing, and people often judge the success of one's work by how many people are saved through it. I'm blessed that my church and the people who have been supporting me financially all these years haven't judged my work in this way. I believe that Jesus looks at success differently, namely by how faithful we are to Him and the things He has told us to do, rather than by how many converts we produce.

Of course, it's always great to see people saved, and Jesus has encouraged me a lot as I have seen a few women receive Him as their Saviour. But I know that according to God's vision, which I shared earlier, I'll only see the majority of the women who have received salvation once we are all standing together in front of His glorious throne. There I'm going to see a multitude of women who used to work in prostitution now dressed in dazzling white robes, worshipping their Saviour Jesus.

Paul was writing to the Corinthian church when he said:

> I planted the seed, Apollos watered it, but God has been making it grow. So neither the one who plants nor the one who waters is anything, but only God, who makes things grow. The one who plants and the one who waters have one purpose, and they will each be rewarded according to their own labour. For we are fellow workers in God's service; you are God's field, God's building.
> *1 Corinthians 3:6-9*

I have an encouraging example of one sowing and another watering the seed which at the time strengthened my faith. Many years ago there used to be a yearly march through London (and other towns and cities) called 'March for Jesus' for which hundreds of Christians would gather and walk and sing through the streets. At one of those events I was introduced to a pastor from the north of England who told me that some time ago a couple had come to his church wanting some advice before getting married. The woman had said she used to work as a prostitute in Soho and that someone called Heidi had visited her. She told him that after that visit she left Soho and never returned. The pastor said they weren't Christians yet, but he was encouraged that they had sought his help and guidance. I have no idea who this woman was, but needless to say I was very uplifted too!

We must also be careful not to uproot the seeds we've been sowing by speaking negative words after visiting or praying. In the Bible we read, 'The tongue has the power of life and death' (Proverbs 18:21). It's very easy to speak out pessimistic words when one is discouraged, and for a long time now I've been asking the Lord to help me keep my mouth shut and say nothing, rather than something unhelpful. It's challenging, especially when there are times when I'm feeling as though I'm being pulled in two directions. On the one hand, I've heard and believed the promises of God, and have seen some of the flats closed and some women's lives changed and transformed. On the other hand, I see corruption and greedy people exploiting the women working in the sex industry, and daily I see young women's lives being wasted while trapped in prostitution, very often through emotional manipulation, empty promises and other evils.

All these things sometimes affect the words I say, my faith and prayer life, and I get tired of praying for God's kingdom to come on earth, here in Soho, as it is in heaven.[14] I remember Jesus encouraging me once on one of my off

---

[14] See Matthew 6:10.

days, when I allowed some injustice to dishearten me. I told Jesus I didn't feel like praying any longer for His righteousness to come in that particular situation, as it was obvious the people involved didn't want to change. Jesus responded that I should never stop asking for His kingdom to come, regardless of the people or the situation.

The Scriptures encourage us, saying, 'Let us not become weary in doing good, for at the proper time we will reap a harvest if we do not give up' (Galatians 6:9). Giving up is giving in to Satan's plans and desires. God's grace is sufficient and will always enable us to 'live by faith, not by sight' (2 Corinthians 5:7) and 'to imitate those who through faith and patience inherit what has been promised' (Hebrews 6:12).

I have very much enjoyed writing this book and looking back on thirty years of sowing, and some reaping. I'm encouraged because I can see everywhere the faithfulness of Jesus. I can see His unconditional love and His amazing grace in many women's lives. I can see it in my own life too; not just in the good seasons but especially in the difficult and disappointing ones.

Hebrews 12:2 inspires us to continue 'fixing our eyes on Jesus, the pioneer and perfecter of faith. For the joy that was set before him he endured the cross, scorning its shame, and sat down at the right hand of the throne of God.' Jesus' joy was to see us, you and me, through His death, coming into a right relationship with His Father, and through His resurrection being 'raised … up … and seated … with him in the heavenly realms' (Ephesians 2:6). Jesus knows 'the end from the beginning' (Isaiah 46:10), and so do we. I don't know in advance the details of my journey with Jesus, but I certainly know the end. I know that one day I will see all God's promises fulfilled, not only the little part I played in His universal plan, but also everything that has been written in His book – 'My purpose will stand, and I will do all that I please' (Isaiah 46:10). May this truth continue to encourage us and make us even more willing to persevere and endure because of the joy that is also set before us!

16. God is Always Working

In a flat where I knew the maid well, the model, a Romanian girl, asked me if I could bring her a Bible, which a team member did a couple of days later. I didn't see her for a few weeks, but when I did I asked her how she was getting on with reading her Bible. She said she couldn't understand very much of what she was reading, but she was going to persevere with it and read it again and again till she could understand better. By then she had already read through the four Gospels and said, 'I can't understand those priests. How could they say that Jesus wasn't God's Son? He opened the eyes of blind people, He made deaf people hear and He put the ear back which Peter had cut off. How could they not believe?' She was very indignant about all those priests who didn't believe Jesus, and it was very refreshing to listen to her!

When the model had to go into the bedroom to serve a client, the maid said that she couldn't take the Bible home as her boyfriend would throw it away, but she was reading it during her time at work when she wasn't busy. Even though the model's situation isn't easy I'm encouraged by the scripture which says, 'so is my word that goes out from my mouth: it will not return to me empty, but will accomplish what I desire and achieve the purpose for which I sent it' (Isaiah 55:11).

One day when I was following up on some of the women I knew, I knocked on a door and, to my surprise, it was opened by a model I didn't know. She invited me in and said that the model I was looking for was ill that day. We talked, and it turned out that she'd worked for eighteen months in another flat in Soho but somehow we'd never met. She told me this was her last day at work before going home to Romania. I asked if she would like me to pray for her and she said that she needed a lot of prayer. I was able to pray for her there and then and give her the *Why Jesus?* booklet. Jesus gave us all the time we needed, and during our conversation and prayer no client knocked on the door, nor did the maid interrupt us, as when I arrived she left the room to finish a conversation on her mobile phone. This visit was indeed a 'Jesus moment', with perfect timing which only He could have orchestrated!

On another occasion on my usual round, I knocked on the door of a flat which, three or four years previously, I used to visit on a regular basis. Not only had the maid been very open to talking, but the model also participated in our conversations. The model was from Eastern Europe, very attractive but very shy and quiet. During those times of visiting I was able to give her something to read about Jesus, and on a couple of occasions I also prayed for her.

Then unfortunately there was a change of maids and from then on I wasn't invited into the flat. The new maid still opened the door when I knocked, to say hi, but she wasn't willing to let me in. This meant I wasn't able to continue the relationship with the model, apart from brief conversations at the door if she happened not to be busy.

This situation continued for a few years until suddenly one day the maid not only opened the door but also invited me in. She started the conversation by saying that she was sorry, but she wasn't interested in religion. I said I wasn't into religion either, but that I had a relationship with Jesus. I explained that I thought it was amazing to be able to have a relationship with the God who created the universe, with someone who was so 'big', yet at the same time was interested in me and my life. She was startled by this idea, listened for a moment and said that she didn't know someone could know God and actually talk to Him. And for about an hour she continued asking me questions!

The model who was working at the flat was still the one I used to know and visit, but she was busy in the bedroom while I was speaking with the maid. When she finished with her client and finally came out, she had just enough time before the next one to tell me that she was leaving the business at the end of the month and was going back home.

On my way out, the maid said I was welcome to come back any time. I continued to visit the flat, and had many interesting conversations about Jesus. After a while, the maid started to share personal family matters and asked if I would pray for her. Remember that just a few months earlier she had said she didn't believe in God! At the time of writing, she hasn't given her life to Jesus, but she does now know that there is a God who loves and cares about her.

The model from Eastern Europe left as she had said she would and returned to her home country. I went on visiting the flat and was introduced to the new model. She was of an Asian background but born in England. In conversation she said she was studying law and was earning her living by working as a prostitute.

On the surface she seemed to be OK with what she was doing and the way she was earning her money. But after visiting the flats in Soho for thirty years I still don't believe that a woman wakes up one morning and says to herself that she's going to earn her living by working as a prostitute. I believe there is always a deeper reason or issue, and I'm certain that each one would have a story to tell.

May Jesus help us to be gracious and not to pass judgement on any woman selling her body, even if it seems she is simply doing it for the money. Only Jesus knows the whole truth, and His desire is for each woman to get to know Him as her personal Saviour and to be restored to know God as her Father and therefore become His precious daughter! The book of Jude tells us vividly, 'Be merciful to those who doubt; save others by snatching them from the fire; to others show mercy, mixed with fear – hating even the clothing stained by corrupted flesh' (verses 22-23). This scripture always reminds me of Jesus' compassion for those who are lost, especially when I'm feeling lazy and would rather be doing something other than knocking on people's doors!

The model from Eastern Europe came back to work after having been away for almost six months. She was very apologetic when we met and said she needed to earn just a bit more money. I could see behind her smile the sadness in her eyes and the pain and disappointment of one more shattered hope and dream.

Despite her situation, and whatever the reasons were for her coming back, she continued to dream. After a few months she said she was going to enrol at a private, well-known college to train as a nursery teacher. To allow time for this she reduced her working days in the flat. It was challenging for her, as she hadn't studied since she had left school, but she persevered and after two years of hard work, she passed all her exams. Shortly after graduating she left her job in Soho, looking forward to a better future.

A while after she had left I sent her a text asking how she was doing. She replied, saying that the text message had made her think about me and that it had made her cry. She thanked me for visiting and praying for her during the years she worked in Soho and commented that my prayers for her not to be working there any longer had finally been answered. She said that she couldn't change the past but certainly her future, and that she was looking forward to living a more fulfilling life!

The message made me cry too. I'll probably never see this beautiful and precious young woman ever again. But I'm comforted by the fact that Jesus knows her by name and that He will continue to send other people across her path.

One of the flats I often visited was a small and dingy place in a basement without windows. It didn't comply with any safety regulations, and if there had been a fire the women would have been trapped. I had good relationships with the maids and the models and they were usually happy to invite me in and chat. Then a few years ago the flat changed hands and a new maid started to work there.

It's rare for a maid in a flat to be hostile to someone visiting from the church. I can understand that because of the nature of the work, not all the sex workers are entirely pleased to see us, but usually after a few months or a year they get used to us and at least open the door for a brief chat. However, this flat proved a difficult place to visit, and we would scarcely be halfway down the stairs to the flat door when we would hear the maid shouting, 'We're busy!' Despite this, we would go down and put flowers or other small gifts by the door. We would have liked to have talked to the model, but in this case it wasn't possible. After quite a while, the maid did open the door on a couple of occasions, but only just wide enough for us to pass her the flowers. The only time she ever opened the door fully was when her little dog escaped through the small opening and was running out to greet my co-workers.

On the face of it, visiting that flat was a waste of time, but with Jesus nothing is ever wasted. I don't know what is going on behind closed doors – nor in the heart of a woman who seemingly has no time for God. Only Jesus knows the whole story, and unless He tells me to stop I will continue to knock on such people's doors even if they remain firmly shut to me. A closed door is no problem for the Holy Spirit, and He is able to minister to people through our prayers without us ever even setting foot in their flats.

I don't know if the flat changed hands or if only the maid changed, but one day when I had finished my visits and was on my way back to the church café, the Holy Spirit stopped me in my tracks. I had the impression Jesus wanted me to make a small detour and visit the basement flat. I was tired and wanted to go home, saying to myself that surely this was all just in my mind. After a couple of minutes I decided the only way to find out if it was me or Jesus was to go there. It would only take a few minutes, and it was worth a try. I was about halfway down the stairs when suddenly the door opened and a familiar voice shouted, 'Heidi, it's so nice to see you again, come in!'

Well, that was a surprise, and I greeted the maid, who used to work in a different flat and whom I hadn't seen for several years, but who obviously still remembered me. We had a happy reunion and chatted away; I also met the model, and before I left the maid told me I was welcome to come back whenever I liked. Isn't Jesus amazing?!

17. A New Generation

There was one Albanian model whom I visited over the course of more than ten years. She was always happy to see me and, no matter how busy she was, she invited me in. Every time I saw her she asked me to pray for her. On some occasions it had to be very quick as one client had just left and another one was already waiting in the bedroom. I wondered sometimes about the effectiveness of those prayers, but in the end I concluded it was up to Jesus to decide if He wanted to listen and answer such prayers.

She too had a boyfriend and after she obtained a British passport they were married in London. She was in love and, like all the other girls, believed that one day they would go back to their home country, be a family and have children. The man was very skilled in his deception and every year he managed somehow to convince her to work for just one more year. This scenario went on and on, and even when there was a rumour that he was living with a younger woman in Albania, she refused to believe it. Once her mother confirmed this to be true but, as I have said earlier, often it seems less painful to believe the lie than face the truth and its consequences.

She continued to work for him for another few years, always believing and saying that even if he had someone else, she was the only one he truly loved. By then he was financially well off and had a business in Albania, where he spent most of his time. They spoke on the phone every day and she continued to give him most of her income, even though she only saw him once or twice a year. The maid frequently urged her to start putting aside some money for herself. She wasn't interested in money but only in how she could make him love her more than he did the other woman. By this time she knew for certain that he had a 'wife' in Albania, and even had two children. As far as I understand, through a conversation with another Albanian friend, it used to be a custom in Albania, still practised at times, for two families to celebrate the marriage of their son and daughter, without necessarily getting it legalised by the state.

The model was in her early thirties when she finally decided to stop working and go back to Albania. She hoped that once she was there, he would leave his 'wife' and children and live with her. We said goodbye and I thought that would be the last time I would see or hear from her.

After a few weeks back in Albania, she called and said she wanted to thank me for always having prayed for her. She said Jesus had shown her that without those prayers she wouldn't have been able to survive! She had also been to a free evangelical church a couple of times, and I really hoped she would find salvation in Jesus.

After she had been back in Albania for a few months she called with the news that she was pregnant. She was in danger of losing the baby and asked for prayer. She said she knew Jesus was going to answer the prayer and help her get through the pregnancy. She had certainly more faith for the situation than I had, but I prayed for her. I knew she had long wanted a baby but, given the circumstances, I doubted that this was such a good idea. After a few months she called again and said that in two days she was going to come back to London. By then she was about seven months pregnant, had no money and nowhere to live. Again, I thought this wasn't such a good idea, but by then I knew her well enough to know that she wouldn't listen and would do what she wanted anyway.

A week later she called from the new place in London where she lived and I went to see her. She was staying in a bedsit and she told me how it had all happened. She said that even though she was pregnant her husband wasn't willing to leave his 'wife' and children. At least not for the time being, he said, and she felt so distraught that she decided to come back to London.

When she had checked in and boarded the flight in Albania, no one noticed that she was heavily pregnant. On the flight she became ill and they arranged for an ambulance to pick her up from the airport. She didn't know at the time, but when Immigration checked her passport and did a police check they noticed that she had worked as a prostitute. In order to keep an eye on her and the unborn child, they arranged for a social worker to visit her at the hospital. That social worker was so efficient that in a couple of days she had arranged a place for her to live and everything else she needed. She truly was a Godsend!

We kept in touch and one day she called to say that she was at the hospital. Her waters had broken but the nurse thought she still had a couple of days before giving birth. I went to visit her, thinking I would stay for a couple of hours and then go back home.

While I was there she had her first labour pains and she asked if I would stay with her till she had the baby. After twenty-four hours she gave birth to a beautiful baby girl.

Her husband did have a bit of a change of heart and he didn't ask her to go on working for him. In fact he said he didn't want the mother of his child working in a brothel. He is providing financially for his daughter and is in regular contact. She still loves him and hopes that one day things will work out for them as a family.

The little girl is now five years old and is the pride and joy of her mother. Her mother wanted her to be brought up in the Christian faith and attend an Anglican school. In order for her to do so, they both had to be baptised. At her baptism she said that this was a very important day for her and that she really wanted to follow Jesus. She did not just want to be baptised so that her daughter could attend the school. My prayer is that mother and daughter will continue to grow in their faith in Jesus and that the little girl's life would be truly blessed.

One of the first women I met in Soho has since become a long-standing friend. When I met her all those years ago she had a small boy but wasn't living with his father. She was engaged to another man and I was invited to their wedding a couple of years later. One of her greatest desires was to have another child with the man she had married, but because of several previous miscarriages it seemed she couldn't carry a baby to full term.

She asked us to pray for her and soon afterwards she became pregnant. She was expecting a girl and we asked Jesus to help her keep the baby. She carried the baby for seven months and then gave birth. When I first visited her in the hospital, the baby was still in an incubator but doing well. My friend asked if I wanted to hold her but I said that I was too scared, as she was so tiny. She lifted her out anyway and she fitted exactly into the palm of my hand. She was a beautiful baby and it has been lovely seeing her grow up.

My friend separated from her husband when her daughter was about eight years old. Their marriage had had its ups and downs, but eventually it broke down completely. A couple of years later, to the surprise of family and friends, her husband moved in with another man. At first it wasn't easy for my friend's daughter to come to terms with her father's decision, but she wanted to continue to see him and visited him on a regular basis at his partner's flat. She did so for several years till one day her father told her that she could no longer visit or see him. He explained to his ex-wife that his partner and daughter didn't see eye to eye and that it was causing a rift in his relationship. He therefore had had to make a choice, and had chosen his partner over his daughter.

This, of course, wasn't an easy time for my friend's daughter and she was very upset and distraught. Sometime later she started to smoke weed, saying that it helped her to relax. I'm not saying the break-up between her and her father was the only reason for her trying out soft drugs, but it certainly didn't help. She wouldn't be the first person I know who started to use soft drugs in order to try to dull the pain and to forget.

A few years after my friend's divorce she met another man who, in my opinion, treated her better than any of her previous partners, and who also looked out for her daughter. Because she was bright and her mother had high hopes for her, he agreed to pay for her to go to a private college. But despite being bright she was still a troubled teenager and was unfortunately expelled.

At the age of eighteen my friend's daughter became pregnant. She and her boyfriend said they wanted to keep the baby and be a family. My friend was positive about the pregnancy and hoped that through it the daughter would become more responsible. As she still lived with her mother she applied to the council and was granted a two-bedroom flat in the same area.

Her mother and partner helped to get the flat ready for the baby's arrival. Soon after, my friend's daughter gave birth to a beautiful baby girl. Sadly, the relationship between the young parents wasn't working. After having lived together for only a few months, my friend's daughter asked her boyfriend to move out. Despite all the problems, my friend and her partner enjoyed their new role as grandparents and helped out as much as they could.

Several months after the baby was born, my friend called me one morning and asked if I could come and see her daughter. Her daughter had phoned, screaming, in the middle of the night, begging her to pick her and the baby up. She said her daughter seemed to have had a bad spiritual experience which was causing her tremendous anxiety and fear. Her daughter had said Jesus was the only one who could help her now, and asked her to call me as I was the only Christian she knew and therefore would know what to do.

I called a pastor colleague local to my friend and daughter, and asked if he would come with me to pray with her. We arranged for her to come and see us at his office. We asked her to leave the baby with her mother so that we would have enough time and space to talk and pray with her. When she arrived she told us her story.

The previous evening she had had some friends at her flat and they were smoking drugs and sharing experiences they had had of the occult. While they were talking, she saw a shaft of light coming towards her and enter her body. She said that she could literally feel the light entering her and taking possession of her. She said that she knew immediately that the light wasn't good but evil. She was so scared by the experience that she told her friends to leave and then immediately called her mother.

She said she now knew the devil was real and she wanted nothing to do with him. She said she was sorry about what she had done and that she wanted to ask Jesus to forgive and help her. We prayed with her and she committed her life to Jesus. Jesus helped her to turn her life around and she stopped smoking drugs and went back to college to continue her education.

I pray that Jesus will complete the work He has started in the life of my friend's daughter, and that her granddaughter, now four years old, would be able to grow up knowing and loving Jesus, and truly be blessed by God!

18. A Turn of Events

In December 2013 the headline of one of the evening newspapers read that the police had launched a blitz on premises in Soho.[15] It went on to say that forty addresses, including twenty-two brothels, had been raided by more than 200 police officers. Twenty-two people were arrested.

The police closed twenty flats during the raids, which reduced our December visits to eighteen flats. A few weeks later some of them reopened, but several remained permanently shut, either by Westminster or their landlord. Many of the models complained about the way they had been treated and exposed in the media.

Two Anglican churches were informed prior to the raid and asked if the models could be brought to their premises. The police wanted to interview the women to find out if any of them had been trafficked or were working involuntarily. This stirred up a lot of controversy and animosity, and a rumour started to circulate that I had known about the raid and was collaborating with the police.

---

[15] See the *Evening Standard*, 5th December 2013, https://www.standard.co.uk/news/crime/22-arrested-as-met-swoops-on-soho-venues-allegedly-linked-to-sex-trafficking-and-rapes-8984378.html, accessed 10th May 2018.

This was not true, as from the very beginning I have always looked at my work as being pastoral and therefore confidential. Many years ago I was asked by someone in the vice squad if I would be willing to help and inform on some people who were making big money by exploiting women in the sex industry. I don't think that this would have been wrong in itself, but the Holy Spirit immediately intervened and reminded me of a verse in the letter to the Ephesians: 'For our struggle is not against flesh and blood, but against the rulers, against the authorities, against the powers of this dark world and against the spiritual forces of evil in the heavenly realms' (Ephesians 6:12). So I declined, saying I didn't feel it was right for me to do so and I've never been asked since.

The rumour caused a lot of difficulty for my team and me, as many madams forbade the maids and the models to let us into the flats. The women who knew me well knew that I hadn't collaborated with the police. But if they happened to work in a flat where the madam had forbidden them to let me in, it meant that I wasn't able to sit with them and have a chat over a cup of tea or coffee. It took more than a year before finally some of the maids and models were allowed to invite me back in, but there are still some flats today which I'm unable to visit because of it.

In one of the flats I was now not permitted to enter, I had good relationships with several maids and models. I would usually have sat with them for an hour or more, talking, and often I would have prayed for them before I left. Nevertheless, I still knocked and brought flowers or other small gifts, and I could ask them about their well-being and pray for them later at home, but it wasn't the same.

The women could always come and see me, of course. Our church café in Soho is within easy walking distance of every flat we visit. But it's very rare that someone ventures out of their flat to visit me. The maids and models come to Soho to work. Once they get to the flat, the only thing that matters is making enough money, first to cover their flat expenses, which are high, and then to earn some for themselves.

As I've mentioned previously, the first flats started to close in 2003, and then little by little until, in 2014, only twenty-five were left open. I was very encouraged by the result of answered prayers. A person once said that I was praying myself out of a job, and it was looking as if one day soon this was actually going to happen.

During 2013, a couple of Chinese businesses offering herbal remedies, acupuncture and massage opened around the corner from our church café. Chinatown and Soho are divided by Shaftesbury Avenue, and until that time there had been only one small Asian food store on our side in Soho, so I was thinking, 'Ah, the Chinese are expanding!' At first I didn't think much of it, but little by little the number of 'herbal shops' increased. Soon it became obvious that they were selling more than just tea. At the time of writing, there are about eight massage parlours on our side of Soho and several more in Chinatown.

In the past, Soho has had many things but, as far as I know, never any massage parlours. I didn't expect this turn of events and I didn't see it coming. It was as if the devil had given his best shot and punched me right in the gut. Its effect knocked me out spiritually and I felt I was dying on the inside. What point was there in the red-light flats closing if instead massage parlours opened up? I felt so depressed and disappointed that it made me want to give up and leave. I think I would have done so, but I had nowhere else to go – or rather, I had no money to go anywhere else, and so I had to stay put.

I didn't want to pray for Soho any more and I told Jesus I couldn't do this any longer, that I was tired, weary and fed up. I was angry and disappointed with Jesus, as He'd allowed it to happen, for what reason I didn't know – and still don't! It took me more than a year to recover from the blow of seeing the massage parlours open up. But even though I was feeling very low, frustrated and on the point of giving up, Jesus continued to be faithful. He brought me through one of the most difficult and painful seasons of my life yet, and I'm very grateful to Him for helping me.

During this difficult and painful year, I continued visiting the flats and the three Thai massage parlours that had opened in a basement a few years earlier. But I tried hard to ignore the Chinese massage parlours and I told Jesus I wouldn't visit them. I kept on saying that visiting them wasn't my job, and that someone else would have to do it. Then one night in December of 2015 I couldn't sleep. Till then I hadn't had a single sleepless night over the massage parlours, but that night they were weighing heavily on my heart and wouldn't shift. I was still awake at five o'clock in the morning when finally I told Jesus I was willing to visit them if He wanted me to.

By then a large Anglican evangelical church had started a new ministry among the massage parlours in Westminster, visiting the ones in Soho every two weeks. I met with the woman who was running the new project and we decided to meet once a month to catch up and pray. I told her the Lord was compelling me to visit the massage parlours on 'my patch', and that I would see them during the weeks they didn't. We agreed that there were plenty of women to follow up without us treading on each other's toes. The two of us are still meeting and praying once a month and it's good to compare notes and be an encouragement to one another.

So, since that sleepless night in December 2015, I've been visiting the Chinese massage parlours as well as the flats. I've been blessed with two lovely co-workers – a mother and her daughter. I met Lucy first when I came to City Gates in 1988. She was then a student but left the church in Soho once she had finished her degree. She joined another Ichthus church, where she met the man who would become her husband. Soon after they were married they moved to Hong Kong, where they lived and worked for ten years before moving to mainland China.

In 2016 they came back to London with their son and daughter, who were about to enrol at university. For the time being, the whole family is living in London, and Lucy and her daughter decided that while they were here they would help me visit the Chinese women.

It's very beneficial to have someone who not only speaks their language, but also knows their culture. Lucy and her daughter have such lovely personalities that many of the women take to them immediately. Lucy kept an open house in China and is used to people coming and going. Here too their home is open, and already she has had one of the Chinese women visit her. She came with her partner and nephew, bringing food to cook a meal at Lucy's house. Lucy said that's what Chinese people do; they're very generous and hospitable!

When we visit the massage parlours we can walk right into the shop. It's not like the flats where one has to knock and wait for the door to open. There are some women who don't speak English, but many of them do, and I can easily converse with them. We usually introduce ourselves by explaining that we're from the local church and that we're offering free English conversation classes. For many years, City Gates Church has been hosting such classes on a Saturday morning in our café in Soho, and they are well attended by many international students. It's an excellent place to go to, it's easy to blend in, and one can meet people from many different countries and nations.

Since we started visiting we have had several Chinese women coming to the classes. Unfortunately, we often lose them again as they are moved around London to work in other parlours. The Chinese have a messaging app similar to WhatsApp, called WeChat, and many have exchanged their WeChat numbers with Lucy. If any of the women need help or want to get in touch they can do so via WeChat, which is a great help. I have been doing a few one-to-ones to help a couple of the women improve their English. I enjoy doing this and it's a simple and practical way to show the kindness and love of Jesus.

I don't think that visiting the massage parlours is my 'new calling', but I felt I should be obedient to Jesus and continue to be faithful on 'my patch', whether the women work in the red-light flats or not. I still don't comprehend why Jesus allowed those parlours to open, but then there are many things I don't understand. One thing, though, I do: no matter what, it's important to remain faithful to Jesus as He always remains faithful to me.

19. What Next?

Recently, Jesus reminded me of a scripture He gave me just a few months after I committed my life to Him: 'I have made you a light for the Gentiles, that you may bring salvation to the ends of the earth' (Acts 13:47). While I was pondering and reflecting on that word, I was suddenly struck by the reality of it and how it has been fulfilling itself without me even noticing! When I first started to visit the women in 1988, the majority were English. But then after about ten years a change took place, and women started to come from Russia and Eastern Europe. During the last thirty years I've also met many women from Thailand, a very few from Kenya and Nigeria, and lately I've been visiting women from China who are working in massage parlours. So, without realising it, I've been 'working' around the world without ever leaving London! Jesus is truly faithful to His promises and He's totally trustworthy and committed to us!

Jesus also reminded me that He didn't just call me to Soho's red-light district to pray for the closure of the flats and the salvation of the women; equally He wants to change and transform my life through the work I am doing. In fact, I believe that Jesus purposefully placed me in Soho primarily to change me more into His likeness. Transformation doesn't happen overnight, and that is one of the reasons why Paul encouraged the Philippian church to 'continue to work out your salvation with fear and trembling, for it is God who works in you to will and to act in order to fulfil his good purpose' (Philippians 2:12-13). To the Corinthian church he wrote, 'And we all, who with unveiled faces contemplate the Lord's glory, are being transformed into his image with ever-increasing glory, which comes from the Lord, who is the Spirit' (2 Corinthians 3:18).

Before moving on to somewhere or something else, I have always wanted to see fulfilled God's promise about the closure of the red-light flats in Soho. I believed that if I didn't stay till its fulfilment I would not only have failed in my ministry, but also in my commitment to Jesus. Right from the beginning I have always been careful not to be distracted or sidetracked by all the many other needs which present themselves so readily in Soho. I learned early on that if I didn't focus on the task I have been set – to reach out to the women in the red-light flats – I could easily be doing lots of good things, but not the things Jesus has told me to do.

In January 2015 I had a ten-day retreat in the Lake District. I have a friend who lives up there who has a small cottage on her property. I've been there several times and it's the perfect place to go and be quiet. One morning during my retreat I woke up thinking that if Jesus asked me to leave Soho and move on to something else, then I wouldn't have failed in my mission. I was reminded of all the promises God made through the prophets in the Scriptures, so many years ago, yet some of them are still not fulfilled. Suddenly the self-imposed burden of having to see something through to its end lifted, and I felt a new freedom, which was very liberating. The thought of perhaps doing something different felt suddenly exciting and exhilarating!

In June 2018 I reached sixty-two, and I don't feel any different from the way I did ten or twenty years ago. When I was pondering where in a few years I should retire to, either England or Switzerland, Jesus said that the word 'retire' isn't found in Scripture. I don't think the Lord meant that it was wrong for me to retire, or that I never should, but this thought certainly challenged me.

One thing I know is that when Jesus comes back (that is, if I'm still here), I would like to be found by Him doing His will and sharing His love with people who do not yet know Him. At present I'm feeling a bit tired and would like to have a break. I recuperate and relax best when I travel and see new places. I thought that maybe I could visit some missionary friends abroad and, while doing so, seek the Lord about the coming years, asking Him what He wants me to do. In Proverbs 3:5-6 we read, 'Trust in the LORD with all your heart and lean not on your own understanding; in all your ways submit to him, and he will make your paths straight.'

I'm happy to stay in Soho for however long Jesus wants me there, but I believe I'm ready for a new adventure. I'm at peace about not yet knowing what the future holds, as I know that my life is securely in God's hands.

On Closing ...

I would like to pray for those of you who don't yet know Jesus as your personal Saviour. I pray that you will know Jesus' unconditional love leading you to give your entire life to Him, confess your sins and receive His forgiveness and cleansing, through His blood poured out for you on the cross of Calvary. I also pray that Jesus would give you the strength to forgive those who have sinned against you, and as you do, you will experience His healing love, cleansing and restoring your soul. I pray that after you have received Jesus as your Saviour, you will know the Holy Spirit filling you and giving you a brand-new life, as you are being restored to your original high calling of being a son or daughter of God the Father, the Creator of this universe. Amen!

If you have received Jesus as your Saviour but don't yet attend church, I would suggest you find yourself a local Christian fellowship where you can be discipled and grow in your faith. If you are already in a church but continue to struggle with some of the issues mentioned in the book, there are two ministries I know of and can recommend:

Journey UK: www.journey-uk.org
Ellel Ministries: ellel.org/uk